Why Should We Teach
About the Holocaust?

Why Should We Teach About the Holocaust?

Edited by
Jolanta Ambrosewicz-Jacobs
Leszek Hońdo

Translated by
Michael Jacobs

Second Edition, expanded

The Jagiellonian University
Institute of European Studies
Cracow 2005

First published in 2003 under the title *Dlaczego należy uczyć o Holokauście?* by the Department of Judaic Studies of the Jagiellonian University in Cracow

First English edition published in 2004 by the Judaica Foundation – Center for Jewish Culture in Cracow, with funding from the Office for Democratic Institutions and Human Rights of the Organization for Security and Co-operation in Europe, Warsaw Office

Second Polish edition published in 2005 by the Institute of European Studies of the Jagiellonian University in Cracow, with funding from the Office for Democratic Institutions and Human Rights of the Organization for Security and Co-operation in Europe, Warsaw Office

This second English edition is published with funding from the Office for Democratic Institutions and Human Rights of the Organization for Security and Co-operation in Europe, Warsaw Office.

The opinions expressed in this publication are those of the authors, and do not necessarily reflect the policies or views of the Office for Democratic Institutions and Human Rights and the Organization for Security and Co-operation in Europe.

Publication coordinator
Anna Motyczka

Cover design
Dorota Ogonowska

Layout
Jan Szczurek

Printing
Drukarnia Leyko, Cracow

Copyright by the Jagiellonian University

ISBN 83-918835-3-1

Foreword to the English Edition

These essays and supplementary material were first published in Polish. This English version of the work is published and distributed thanks to funding from the Office for Democratic Institutions and Human Rights of the Organization for Security and Co-operation in Europe.

The editors are grateful for this OSCE support, and hope that this edition will bring new insights to the European discussion of Holocaust education. The book is also intended to demonstrate the range of interest in the subject in Poland. Knowing, writing, talking and teaching about the Holocaust are integral to the work of people in fields as diverse as classroom teaching, religious ministry, psychotherapy, the media, and a host of academic professions here. It could not be otherwise, since that tragic chapter is integral to our history. The reasons our contributors give for the need to teach about the Holocaust should serve as pointers to the spheres of national life in which the subject requires greater exposure. The larger context of the task, and the larger imperative, are implied by the fact of OSCE sponsorship of this publication.

Jolanta Ambrosewicz-Jacobs

Introduction

This collection of essays, supplemented by a section describing institutions that have educational tools at their disposal, was compiled for readers for whom the teaching/learning process is an open one, not necessarily limited to fixed teacher-student roles. The book is addressed to people who are not indifferent to the fact of the murder of ten percent of the citizens of prewar Poland, and also to people who may not have realized this yet.

Authorities in public life and specialists in various academic fields were invited to contribute the essays published here. Among them are a philosopher, anthropologist, literary historian, psychologist, journalist, ethnographer, theologian, cultural historian, political scientist, high school teacher, sociologists and historians. Many of the authors refer to their own memories, their experiences from the places where they were born, which are connected with Jewish and Romani life and with the Holocaust (Bełżec, Tarnów, Czarna Góra, Warsaw). They recall encounters with people whose wise and sympathetic attitudes are etched in memory (Rabbi Jules Harlow, Rabbi Jacob Baker). Not all the authors have ready answers about how to perpetuate that memory. All are deeply aware of the need for education about the Holocaust, for the sake of reconciliation between nations, democracy and peace.[1]

---

[1] "Holocaust" originally meant a burnt offering. Presently the term is most often used in reference to the Nazi mass murder of Jews during World War II. Among Jews, "Shoah" is often the preferred term. After all, burnt offerings were sacrifices made to God in biblical times, and the massacre of innocents cannot be compared to a form of worship of the Lord.

Teaching about the Holocaust is not only a matter of teaching facts, although reliable knowledge, the lack of which often leads to arrogance and prejudice, is of great importance. It is important to comprehend the meaning of those facts, to cultivate empathy and sensitivity. That is why many of the essay writers refer to personal experiences and reflections on the place where they live.

No set criterion was applied to the choice of authors. Thus, the names of many eminent experts on the period and specialists on the Holocaust are missing. The selection was guided by the editors' personal acquaintance with the authors. We know that they engage with Holocaust subjects and that their involvement translates to specific educational activities (creating new units at educational institutions and within NGOs, international pilot programs, teaching, writing for the general public, therapeutic work).

Jerzy Tomaszewski retrieves pages of the shared Polish-Jewish past in order to show that the Jewish Holocaust meant not only the loss of Polish citizens but the impoverishment of our cultural identity. Zdzisław Mach stresses that for the younger generation the issue of the Holocaust and Polish-Jewish relations is critical to the shaping of a new historical identity. Invoking his own memories of 1968, Ireneusz Krzemiński speaks of how organized hatred acts within a person, and what havoc it wreaks in society.[2] Bohdan Michalski wishes to demythologize Polish knowledge of the Holocaust. Stanisław Krajewski ends his essay by saying that everywhere there is a need to teach how the sowing of contempt can lead to killing. For Reverend Stanisław Obirek, the memory of the murdered citizens of Tomaszów Lubelski and Narol should be incorporated into the collective memory of his native region. Tanna Jakubowicz-Mount focuses

---

[2] 1968 was the year of the "March events," a Communist Party-led anti-Semitic campaign in which many Jews were removed from their government and professional posts, and Jews were pressured to leave the country.

her attention on the identity crisis and on the mechanisms leading to violence here and now, illustrating her point with a description of stages of self-exploration. She outlines the phases of a program to teach about the Shoah. Stefan Wilkanowicz emphasizes that the methods of fanning hatred and aggression are similar in every tragedy (Auschwitz, Kolyma, Sarajevo, Cambodia, Rwanda), although each calamity has its particular, unique features. For the evil not to be repeated, he advises us to take advantage of the potential in young people who want to oppose evil, because they can be teachers to their peers. In his reflections as a teacher, Robert Szuchta discusses in detail the situation in the Polish school system, NGO projects, how to teach about the Holocaust, and the difficulties that are faced. For Sergiusz Kowalski the goal is to purge history of falsehood, particularly since the methodologies of classroom teaching and catechesis are not keeping up with public discussion about reconstructing the collective memory. Olga Goldberg-Mulkiewicz demonstrates that folk art replicating the stereotype of the Jew does not incorporate the problem of the Holocaust in any way. Monika Adamczyk-Garbowska shares her experiences from teaching practice, quoting statements from college students whose high school education had taught them little of the life, history, culture and tragedy of the Jewish people. This finding is seconded by Hanna Węgrzynek, who says that she did not learn about the Holocaust of Warsaw's prewar citizens until her university studies. Leszek Hońdo points to the moral dimension and the universal experience of what happened to the Jews, stressing that the continued use of the word "Jew" as an expletive argues for the need to teach about the Holocaust. In his essay, Sławomir Kapralski says that it is worthwhile and necessary to teach about the Holocaust of the Roma because we owe it to them; besides meeting the ethical need for discussion of the moral implications of recognizing Roma as victims of Nazi persecution, it also provides an opportunity to reflect on how memory functions in the process of creating and maintaining group identity. Andrzej Mirga reminds us that in the Nuremberg trials the question of the Romani Holocaust was addressed marginally. He shows how the memory of the genocide against Roma is gradually becoming a part of the institutionalized memory of the Holocaust, and stresses that it is absent from the school curricula and, in turn, from the historical memory of postwar generations. For Natalia Aleksiun, a member of the younger generation of researchers, the efforts by Jews, even as they faced their imminent fate, to preserve the memory of their plight under German occupation, constitutes a moral challenge to convey this truth. For all the authors, the memory of the atrocities, and the form of that memory, is important for current and future generations, if we are to be able to oppose prejudice and discrimination here and now, and to prevent their recurrence.

New ways of conveying knowledge of the Holocaust are needed so that succeeding generations of Poles will not have the same attitude to the Holocaust that they do to the Napoleonic Wars. Our authors remind us that racism, xenophobia and genocide occur amidst us, and the memory of the Holocaust should serve as a warning against the repetition of crimes against humanity.

In addition to the scholars, editors, teachers and organizers of various educational projects who wrote articles for this book, Jagiellonian University students also contributed by preparing a practical guide to Internet sites devoted to teaching about the Holocaust, for readers who wish to learn how others (mainly academic institutions and NGOs) approach the task in different parts of the world such as Western Europe, the United States and Poland.

If not for the particular pursuits of Jagiellonian University students, this book would not have appeared. These members of the "third generation" undertook studies connected with the history and culture of Polish Jews, usually without knowing why, unable to explain their interest rationally. They pursued these studies as part of course work in the Jagiellonian

University's Research Center on the History and Culture of the Jews in Poland or else outside the framework of that interdisciplinary research unit.[3]

With time, students have increasingly taken up subjects related to the Holocaust and to the attitudes of Poles to Jews before, during and after the war, topics which for almost half a century were taboo in academia and in public life. No one forced these difficult and painful subjects on the students. Coming from different parts of Poland to study in Cracow, often it was here that they learned about the Jewish minority which the war years eliminated from Poland's social landscape. Few schoolteachers were able to say anything about the Holocaust, the pogroms, or Jewish emigration from Poland after 1946 or after 1968.[4]

Teachers also contributed to this work. Teachers interested in the methodology of teaching about the Holocaust took part in several conferences at the Center for Jewish Culture in the Kazimierz district of Cracow, organized by the Spiro Institute of London jointly with Polish institutions. The number of teachers wanting to attend the Kazimierz conferences exceeded the number of places available. They were faced with a lack of teaching materials. Piotr Trojański and Robert Szuchta published the first Holocaust curriculum for Polish secondary schools in 2000, and the first textbook in 2003.[5] Some of the Internet sites we describe can provide other materials.

With increasing knowledge about the Holocaust victims and the consequent "depolonization" of the associated memorial sites, fewer young

---

[3] The Center, created by Professor Józef A. Gierowski, is now the Department of Judaic Studies. On October 2, 2001, Poland's first such major program was inaugurated in the Department.

[4] 1946 was the year of the "Kielce pogrom" in which 41 Jews were killed.

[5] R. Szuchta, P. Trojański, *Holocaust. Program nauczania o historii i zagładzie Żydów na lekcjach przedmiotów humanistyczny w szkołach ponadpodstawowych*, Warsaw 2000; R. Szuchta, P. Trojański, *Holokaust. Zrozumieć dlaczego*, Warsaw 2003.

people have been visiting the Auschwitz-Birkenau State Museum.[6] Is it possible that we were interested exclusively in sites of national martyrdom? Do the numbers or numerical proportions reduce the significance of the genocidal crimes? Does the fact that "only" 75,000 Poles perished in Auschwitz, and almost a million Jews, lessen what Auschwitz means to Poles? Auschwitz is a place and symbol of genocide important to all humanity, and particularly to Poles because it was Polish soil that the Nazis selected to be a site of the Holocaust. The genocide took place amidst us, before our eyes. That is why it should be taught, in the knowledge that if we pass over those difficult and painful events in silence, our children and grandchildren may ask us about them. It should be taught if only because 88 percent of a national sample of 1,002 surveyed 16-year-olds declared that "knowledge of the crimes perpetrated at Auschwitz and other concentration camps should be conveyed to the next generations as a lesson for all mankind."[7]

Professor Feliks Tych of the Jewish Historical Institute in Warsaw gives the information that 95 percent of the Poles survived the German occupation, while 98 percent of the Polish Jews were murdered during it.[8] This difference in the fates of Poles and Jews should also be taught, because Polish youth are not fully aware of it, as demonstrated by the survey referred to here, conducted ten years after the collapse of a system that

---

[6] This information came from Alicja Białecka, a staff member at the Museum, during the Education for Reconciliation workshop held at the Grodzka Gate NN Theater Center in Lublin on May 16–18, 2001, organized by the Carnegie Council of New York and the Jagiellonian University's Department of Judaic Studies. After 2000, the number of visits began to increase gradually. Demographic and economic factors, and the reform of the school system, have also affected the dynamic of visits to the Auschwitz Museum; see: M. Kucia, "Visitors to the Auschwitz-Birkenau State Museum," *Pro Memoria*, January 2004, no. 20, pp. 39–43.

[7] Research findings on attitudes toward the Holocaust are presented in the last article in this book.

[8] F. Tych, "Shoah pamięć zagrożona," *Znak* 2000, no. 6, pp. 55–62.

falsified the historical truth: 24.5 percent of the 1,002 students agreed with the statement that the Jews suffered the most during the war, 20 percent disagreed, and the majority, 55.5 percent, answered "hard to say." Many respondents chose evasive answers to the questions about attitudes to the Holocaust. This could be the result of a lack of information, but in some cases, particularly with the difficult questions such as those about the help extended to Jews, it could represent an attempt to reduce the tension associated with uncertainty about how one's own family members acted. To avoid topics, questions and problems is not to resolve them, but only to push them aside, to make them taboo. No one is to blame for this. It is a phenomenon characteristic of victims who do not want to return to their trauma. However, there comes a time when the inner need is to confront the past, and this can apply to individuals, societies, nations, states. In recent years this need has increased and has expressed itself in different forms: research on subjects missing from or else falsified in the history textbooks of many countries, efforts related to compensation claims, and voices demanding justice, if only symbolic justice in the form of official apologies. It is a global process involving many issues: the lack of compensation for slavery in the United States, discrimination against aboriginal people in Australia, corporate profits from forced labor during the occupation, and banks' silence about frozen accounts in countries traditionally considered neutral. Poland should not be outside this process of confronting a difficult past, if only because we need deep reconciliation with other peoples and states, just as we need a deep, not a superficial democracy, a democracy cognizant of the need to address the marginalized as well as the obvious issues of history and society.[9]

---

[9] "Deep democracy" is a term used by the process-oriented psychologist Arnold Mindell; see: A. Mindell, *Sitting in the Fire: Large Group Transformation Using Conflict and Diversity*, Portland, Oregon 1997.

Jerzy Tomaszewski

Why...

1

In the Commonwealth of Two Nations in the 18th century, about 80 percent of all the world's Jews lived, worked, and participated in the life of the whole country.[10] In the Republic of Poland in 1939, almost 3.5 million Jews lived, worked, and took part in the life of the nation and local communities.

Jewish settlement on our soil dates back to nearly the beginnings of the Polish state. Along with other new arrivals invited by Polish monarchs, Jews played a vital role in the development of cities, trade, crafts and various arts in the Middle Ages; on the first coins of the Polish kings, the name of King Mieszko was stamped in Hebrew letters. When the Commonwealth experienced its golden age, Jews benefitted as well, though there was no lack of instances of persecution, absurd accusations, and above all contempt and suspicion toward Jews as the "faithless ones" who had inherited the blame for Christ's crucifixion. In the period of the Commonwealth's decline, the Jews suffered as well, and often at times of danger they defended the cities together with the other townspeople.

In the 18th and 19th centuries they played an outstanding role in the development of the country's modern economy, and frequently joined in with their countrymen in the fight for freedom and independence: in uprisings under the command of Tadeusz Kościuszki, in the 1863 insurrec-

---

[10] The Commonwealth of Two Nations included large areas of present-day Eastern Europe, including Poland and Lithuania.

tion, and in Józef Piłsudski's Legions. They lost their lives in the ranks of Polish units on every front of World War II.

2

The Jews who settled on the lands of the Polish state brought with them traditional forms of religious community organization, the rich traditions contained in the Old Testament, and an original culture which they developed further in the new homeland. It was here that in the 19th century the Jewish folk language evolved and assumed its finished form – Yiddish, graced with the Nobel Prize awarded to Polish-born Isaac Bashevis Singer, whose works are dominated by themes drawn from the shared Jewish-Polish tradition. In the first half of the 20th century, Jewish literature developed in the Polish language as well, and a teacher from the Ukrainian-Polish-Jewish town of Drohobycz, the writer and artist Bruno Schulz, became world-renowned. He was murdered by a Nazi on the streets of his home town.

It is hard to overestimate the mutual influence of Polish and Jewish cultures. The Bible, born in Jewish Palestine, has influenced Polish culture since earliest times. In the 19th and 20th centuries the works of Jewish authors writing in Polish had a significant influence, and Poland's most eminent poets and prose writers include the names of Poles from Jewish families. There are Jewish motifs in the most celebrated works of Polish literature, including *Master Thaddeus* by Adam Mickiewicz. In turn, Polish motifs run through many works of Jewish literature; for Shalom Ash the waters of the Vistula murmured in Yiddish. Similar links can be seen in other works of art.

3

We observe many Polish-Jewish ties in the world of politics, beginning from the institution of the Council of Four Lands (*Va'ad arba aratzot*), modeled after the unmistakable design of the Polish-Lithuanian Sejm in the Commonwealth of Two Nations.[11]

The so-called emancipation of the Jews in the 19th century, that is, their achievement of equal civil rights (though with certain exceptions, especially under Russian rule), created the conditions for Jews to participate in political life on an equal footing with other residents of the partitioned Polish lands. They served in local and regional government bodies wherever they were formed. In November 1918, Józef Piłsudski as head of state invited representatives of the largest Jewish parties for consultations on forming the Republic's government. Jewish deputies and senators were part of the sovereign state's legislature, shared in making laws, and took part in the debates. They also bore the consequences of this; one of them, Warsaw University professor Rabbi Mojżesz Schorr, was placed in a Soviet camp in the autumn of 1939, where he died. The experiences of those years influenced the shaping of some of the State of Israel's legal and political institutions in 1948; one of the members of its first Provisional Council of State was Yitzhak Gruenbaum, previously a deputy to the Republic of Poland's Sejm.

4

Probably not quite ten percent of the Jews who lived in Poland survived the Second World War, mostly outside Poland's borders. The losses among the other people living on Polish soil – losses resulting from warfare, the conditions in Nazi and Soviet camps, and murders committed in other circumstances – probably amounted to about ten percent.

The Jewish Holocaust was planned and decided in Berlin, and carried out by institutions and functionaries of the Third Reich. Polish soci-

---

[11] Council of Four Lands: the central institution of Jewish community self-government in Poland in the 16th to 18th centuries.

ety, subjected to a brutal occupation regime, had no part in those decisions and no influence on their implementation. The majority, living under the threat of the occupier's terror, remained passive witnesses, often feeling concern but powerless to act. Some, unfortunately too few, did assist the persecuted, either in organized ways through the Council for Aid to Jews or else on their own.[12] They saved the honor of the Poles. There were those, however, who betrayed hidden Jews and their protectors to the occupier, and even committed murder themselves. We still know little about those dismal pages of the Holocaust.

5

After 1945, some of the few Polish Jews who survived the Holocaust tried to rebuild the Jewish community in Poland. Others undertook to leave Poland, to enter Palestine in order to join in building the Jewish state or else to avoid repeating the experience of the communist system they had known in the Soviet Union. Soon it became clear that in the system created by the communists there was no chance to reconstruct independent Jewish life; what is more, the internationalist sloganeering did not preclude anti-Semitism. The number of Jews remaining in Poland decreased as repeated waves of anti-Jewish feeling were stirred up by infighting within the ruling party in 1957 and 1968. Today only a few thousand Jews remain in Poland; despite their tragic experiences they continue to cultivate their traditions, which are tightly bound up with Polish traditions. Likewise, Polish culture, and not only its literature, preserves ineradicable traces of Jewish influences, and the memory of centuries of shared destinies and shared existence on the same land.

---

[12] Żegota, the Council for Aid to Jews, was a clandestine organization in occupied Poland, under the auspices of the Polish government in exile.

6

The history of Poland cannot be presented without the history of the Polish Jews, as it cannot be presented without the history of the other religious and ethnic communities inhabiting a common state whose territory has changed through the millennium. Polish culture cannot be understood without at least a rough knowledge of Polish-Jewish relations. The Jewish Holocaust during the occupation was the most tragic fragment of the shared past. We lost not only fellow citizens but also an important element of our cultural identity.

To learn and understand the causes of the catastrophe, and how Polish-Jewish relations were shaped in those years, is not only a moral obligation to our murdered neighbors. It is also a duty to Polish culture and tradition, to our future. The Holocaust came from the outside, but whether and how society was prepared for this test of attitudes and conscience remain open questions. In the Christian Bible, part of which is also the Jewish Torah, the question is asked, "Where is Abel thy brother?" We must not repeat the reply, "Am I my brother's keeper?" It is a question facing the other communities of Europe as well.

7

The murder of the Jewish people was a tragedy on a scale unknown in the 20th century. It would be naive to delude ourselves that a similar catastrophe cannot be repeated in one or another region of our continent, or outside Europe. Learning and understanding the sources of the Holocaust may give us a chance to avert a similar tragedy in the future.

Zdzisław Mach

The Memory of the Holocaust and Education for Europe

History and consciousness are dimensions of Poland's political transformation. Poles are experiencing a serious identity crisis. They must rethink and debate questions connected with their place in the history of Europe, and their relations with their neighbors and with the peoples who were significant partners in their history. Mythologized history has been an instrument for creating national identity, and an inexhaustible source of the symbols with which the image of the social world is constructed. History was subordinated to ideology particularly in the 19th century, and in Poland between the world wars and through the whole period from 1945 to 1989. In the process of building a democratic civil society, Poland now must above all deal with historical moments that in the recent past were taboo topics or were particularly distorted by political and historical ideology.

The search for a new interpretation of our history involves the need to purge it of ideology, to reconsider it, and to find in it a new meaning better suited to a democratic civil society. Of great importance in this are the processes of globalization and European integration – Poland's incorporation into supranational structures – and along with this the imperative to find a broader perspective, one no longer dominated by the notions of the nation and the nation state. Whatever role the nation state plays in a future Europe, in people's consciousness it will coexist with other forms of collective identity, and the construction of supranational identities will entail linking the meaning of national histories to broader, universal values, and to the history of Europe and the world.

Teaching history in a rapidly changing world will demand rethinking the meaning of not only the most important social processes but also events that hold particular symbolism. The Holocaust is one such event which defines the contemporary culture of Europe and exerts a huge influence on the image of the social world.

The Holocaust is often and rightly described as the most tragic moment in Europe's history, the culmination of what is worst in European civilization: intolerance, hatred of strangers, genocide. This event touches Poland and the Poles in a particular way. The Holocaust unfolded largely on Polish soil and in the presence of Poles. The nature of that presence continues to be a much-discussed and very controversial matter. Some speak of the Pole's co-responsibility or co-guilt, and it is by no means only moral responsibility that they have in mind. Others state that the Poles' share of blame lies basically in indifference, silent assent motivated by estrangement from the Jews or else by outright anti-Semitism. Still others wonder whether Poles could have done more to aid the Jews who were being murdered, and why they did not. In every case the position taken and the answer given require very serious consideration of many aspects of the question. The background is Polish society in the past, composed of Jews as well as Poles, the Catholic and the Jewish religions, and the moral and social values of European culture. For the young generation, dealing with the problem of responsibility for the Holocaust and the role of Poles, whatever it was, is a precondition for rebuilding their own historical identity. It is not only a matter of establishing the facts, or even of doing justice to those who died rescuing Jews, those who looked on indifferently, or those who often directly or indirectly derived benefits from the Holocaust. Equally important is to reconsider the history of

Polish-Jewish relations, which arrived at their tragic finale in the Holocaust. Of course the point here is not collective responsibility but rather knowledge and understanding of one's history and relations with other nations and groups, and from this point of view Polish-Jewish relations are of special significance.

To teach about the Holocaust means first of all to convey the truth about the events, and to give them an interpretation that incorporates on the one hand the state of people's consciousness at that point in history, and on the other hand our moral and social views today. Secondly, teaching about the Holocaust means shaping the collective historical memory. In the past, many things were erased from this memory, and many things distorted. In communist postwar Poland the imperative was to mold a uniform group consciousness and identity for the Poles, one congruent with a socialist and nationalist vision of the world. Tolerance and cultural pluralism were not among the values the rulers wanted to support. Poland's history was presented in a way that could promote the ideal of a monocultural society, ethnically pure, uniform in every regard. Traces of other cultures were eliminated from social consciousness, from curricula, and from the official images of cities and regions. Jewish cemeteries, synagogues and other preserved relicts were marginalized and forgotten. The Holocaust itself was subordinated to the official state ideology, which was dominated by anti-Semitism after 1968. Now, in building a pluralistic society and developing openness and tolerance, we must restore these relicts to their rightful place, and above all speak of the Jews' contribution to Polish culture and of the presence of an extraordinarily rich Jewish culture in Polish society. Thirdly, then, to teach about the Holocaust means to recall the role of Jews in Poland and in Polish culture, and to make clear the irreparable loss that the Holocaust inflicted on Polish society, eliminating three million citizens and their achievements. Fourthly, to teach about the Holocaust means to warn of a danger. Intolerance, xenophobia and anti-Semitism have not died out in Europe. Often they are said to be intensifying. They are present in Poland as well. To show the Holocaust in all its dimensions is to give a warning.

To sum up: to teach about the Holocaust is to inculcate the idea of a pluralistic society, to show what intolerance and an ideology of racial purity can lead to, and to forge attitudes that encourage the building of a new, shared, pluralistic, open and tolerant Europe, and within it a Poland capable of dealing with its legacy.

Ireneusz Krzemiński

In Light of Later History

The year was 1967. Warsaw, the start of winter, early evening, the corridor in the university's Philosophy Department building at the corner of Krakowskie Przedmieście and Traugutta Streets. A colleague, Andrzej S., was launching into an explanation of how naive it was to believe what my friends Irena and Helena said.

> "After all, they're Jews!" he said forcefully, looking at me with an ironic smile.
> "So what?" I protested. It was all new to me, and made no sense.
> "What, don't you know? You can't ever trust the Jews, because they've always got something in mind different from what they're saying – their own interests, which we have no idea of!"
> "What are you talking about? I hear what they say. We've been having discussions for months, so why shouldn't I believe it?"
> "You shouldn't trust them. You're naive to want to be friends with them. You'll see," he said, and handed me an envelope.

In it I found a packet of pages explaining the evil of Jewish Zionism and spelling out the plainest anti-Semitic accusations. A few months later he was in the Communist Party avant-garde, opposing the protesting student body.

If I attempt the device of recalling that conversation, it is because it struck me with a sense of astonishment that persists to this day. What sprang from my interlocutor was, at the least, animosity – personal animosity toward our fellow students! The discussions referred to were taking place at the university in a series of student forums. Long before the premiere of *Dziady* and the subsequent March protest, the atmosphere at school had been full of social and political ferment, and fiery discussion.[13] Generally it was about the scope of freedom in public life, freedom of expression and association, and whether it was acceptable to restrict them. Two different positions clearly emerged, which in the language of those days can be expressed this way: the first favored democratization or, as it was put, liberalization, continuation of October '56; the second maintained that it was necessary to unite with the Party and to be mindful of the national interest, which was a novelty in socialist rhetoric. We eighteen-year-olds, entering adult life though it was still student life, had these discussions on our minds. They were extraordinarily important to us.

I have remembered that conversation my whole life. The memory has flooded in many times, to serve as an illustration of an attitude of hatred, the attitude of *organized hatred*. Because here some abstract outlook, a social outlook, it would seem, a social stereotype, had completely determined how particular living people were seen. The categorization, the label "they're Jews!" had completely decided my colleague's personal attitude to our companions, real people, who differed from each other. More than that: for at least one of them, as for me too, the term "Jew" meant little. And yet, the identification attached to her determined the entire way in which everything that occurred between her and my hating colleague was interpreted. It was a disinterested attitude, in which the hatred was wholly independent of the actual, concrete acts and views of the hated person. The moral judgement was ascribed to her as a representative of a *social category*.

---

[13] The student protests that preceded the anti-Semitic campaign of 1968 came after the authorities closed down a staging of Adam Mickiewicz's dramatic poem *Dziady*.

Later on, the conversation I have quoted found its much broader, one can say sociopolitical, extension in the form of an organized anti-Semitic campaign by the Party and the state, emerging officially under the slogan of anti-Zionism. Zionism was seen as an almost mystical threat to the nation and – to socialism! This has determined my outlook on life, for my whole life, basically. It has directed me to seek, in sociological knowledge and sociological research, an ally against the thing my conversation with my colleague S. made me aware of, and horrified me with. For scientific knowledge cannot foster hatred, cannot aid in organizing people's thinking and actions against other people. Knowledge must not only allow the psychological mechanisms of hatred to be elucidated, but must also encourage a view of the world that will permit us to make judgements not through the prism of preconceived, socially sanctioned prejudices and ideological simplifications.

Knowledge of the Second World War, including the singular slaughter of the Jews, was an essential article for my whole generation. Weren't we brought up on war films, and on hate-filled indictments of Nazi Germany and fascism for all the world's evil – from which socialism was supposed to bring salvation, of course. These were ever-present in propaganda and in history lessons. As early as primary school days I belonged to the History Club, and recent history interested me the most. One of the things on the wall of my room was a map of Poland with the concentration camps and death camps marked on it. But it was the experience of March 1968 that added a new dimension, as it were, to the school learning of those days. It showed that this ideologically organized hatred was not only the reality of fascist Germany.

The Holocaust can be seen as a kind of culmination of such organized hatred: hatred organized around national feeling, but also around a plan for a better world, justified on nationalist and racist grounds. There is no doubt that the Holocaust was the culmination of ideological hatred for Jews, the culmination of the ideological anti-Semitism that had penetrated European life since the French Revolution, and which reinforced – in the modern language of politics – the old Christian anti-Semitic heritage. In this sense, then, teaching about the Holocaust means demonstrating the historical consequences of a phenomenon present in different forms in the traditions of all of Europe, with its cultural and religious diversity, or it means at least reflecting upon how that evil heritage promoted the Holocaust.

Teaching about the Holocaust means something more, however, because without that particular form of German Nazi racism the Holocaust would have been impossible. It would have been impossible to carry out the Holocaust as a social enterprise solely on the basis of anti-Semitism, even rabid anti-Semitism, whether it be the contemporary ideological form or the traditional religious form. For that enterprise a new political ideology was needed, one combining anti-Semitic content with a racial national mythology and subordinating it to a project for a totalitarian new world. The Nazi ideology of the Holocaust particularly deserves study and recollection, because the menace it presented was assembled from many different European and German strands, from a rich tradition, to create a lethal weapon. To racism and a racial national mythology it was necessary to add the populism of a totalitarian project for a supposedly *better* arrangement of the world. This allowed the Jews to be stigmatized, just as the capitalist and feudal "exploiters" were stigmatized in that other – communist – totalitarian project. More than that, the blueprint for a better new world allowed the Jews to be excluded from the human family, from that part of humanity worth building the new life for. Realization of the totalitarian ideal required the elimination of threatening "elements" from humanity: the Jews in the German Nazi version, the exploiters of the proletariat in the Russian communist version.

Let us note, then, how important it is to have comprehensive education about this crime of the 20th century. First, it tells how religion can degenerate into such evil and dangerous social prejudices, how people's deepest religious feelings can succumb to truly diabolical perversion. Second, it is the most shocking example of the workings of ideology, ideology as a system of comprehending the world but also as a system for programming collective and individual life. The kind of organization that shapes how people look at the world, and which penetrates, it would seem, into the depths of intimate emotions, stripping man of his own individual mental and moral strengths. Third and finally, it is an example of the special evil of the 20th century, an evil inseparably bound up with politics, exploiting the deep human desire to live in a better world, placing that desire in service to a denial of human freedom and dignity, in service to the ruin of the entire European tradition, the culture that created the individual person.

From the perspective I adopt here, the Holocaust was the central aspect of a truly satanic enterprise designed in the 20th century, an enterprise to build a *new world* and, of course, a *new man*. The Holocaust was the mass killing of Jews, which cannot be forgotten, but that attempt to physically annihilate all of Jewish society was also an attack on the whole tradition and civilization of Europe. It was an attempt not only against the sum of human achievement, but against God, without whom that culture certainly would not have taken shape. That is why the memory of the Jewish Holocaust is and should be the memory of the spiritual tradition from which we come, from which even secular Europe comes, however much it has treated that tradition as the distant past. The point is that both of those totalitarian enterprises of the 20th century were aimed at disinheriting the *new societies* and the *new people* of memory and tradition, so that they would become like a wave propelled by the leaders of their parties and activated by feelings hostile toward *others*.

There is still another issue linked to the memory of the Holocaust, and relevant not only in Poland but also in the societies of Eastern Europe only recently living in freedom: the issue of the enormity of suffering that the Second World War brought, and the experience of two inhuman totalitarian systems. The complicated experiences of Polish people show, on the one hand, the extent to which traditional anti-Semitic attitudes (both religious and political/ideological) assisted the crimes of the German Nazis; on the other hand, they show that anti-Semitism as ritualized animosity toward Jews had to be surpassed for it to become a system of crime. The paradox in the reality of occupied Poland was that people with anti-Semitic attitudes helped create and provide organized aid to Jews. At the same time, education about the Holocaust in Poland must make clear the extent to which people's ideological baggage, which the anti-Semitic pre-war National Democrats had given them, made them resemble the key actors, the German murderers, spiritually, psychologically, and sometimes actively (as in the case of Jedwabne and that whole region).

National feeling has to be suspended here if we are to come to terms with the villainy in our tradition, not in order to forget our nation but in order to see it better and to love it with more wisdom. Particularly since in Poland the memory of the Holocaust should mean – again perhaps paradoxically – recovering the memory of the presence of the Jewish world in Polish social life, in Polish history, and above all in Polish culture. Even today it is difficult to imagine Jewish culture, that in Israel and that in America, without what it took from the centuries of its existence in Poland, without the influence of Polish culture. All the more difficult to imagine Polish culture without the contribution of outstanding creative people who were at once Polish and Jewish. The point is for the memory of the Jewish Holocaust to bring a sense of community, and not rivalry about who really "suffered more." In this lies the whole trouble in teaching honestly about the appalling past: in Poland those particular, specific crimes of Nazi Germany have to be presented in very accurate detail, because Poles also suffered a great deal on this bloody soil. In making clear the specific plan of Nazi Germany and the enormity of destruction and suffering dealt the Jews, the commonality between that suffering and the suffering of Poles, Ukrainians, Lithuanians, Russians and others must be shown. Teaching about that atrocity should change young people's view of the world: care must be taken so that organized hatred cannot in any way take hold in them.

Bohdan Michalski

Let's Teach All of It from the Start

Basha, little Barbara, is reading ghetto memoirs and weeping: this is the scene her mother has recalled, and in this reading matter she sees the source of her daughter's huge problems in adolescence. Basha has decided to be a Jewess, and has begun a search for her imagined Jewish ancestors. Why wasn't sensitive Basha allowed to grow up in peace, and why were her loving parents transformed, in her mind, into enemies concealing her fantasized Jewish roots from her? Why must our children, the third postwar generation, have to undergo the torment of assigned reading of Holocaust books?

Since unfortunately we cannot, I believe, spare them the shocking truth about the century of the "mystery of evil," knowledge that is even beyond the endurance of adults, let us proceed cautiously so that the knowledge will not damage them but will, like a vaccination, immunize them against evil. Is that possible? I don't know. In Holocaust education the outcomes are unknown, after all; only the aim is clear. We teach so that genocide on a mass scale, the specialty of the past century, can be circumvented in the future.

A precondition for peaceful coexistence between groups with different identities, that is, different cultures, histories or religions, is tolerance. The political precondition of tolerance, as practice teaches, is democracy. Thus it would seem to be a matter of inculcating in our children the conviction that the only guarantee of avoiding the tragic experiences of both

33

totalitarian systems lies in democratic mechanisms. But is democracy really the panacea for intolerance? Unfortunately, not entirely. In democratic Poland we are still intolerant. We don't like Jews, Russians, Gypsies, Romanians and Germans. In the democratic United States there are outbreaks of strong ethnic conflict every so often, the democratic French can't stand Arabs, and the Germans can do without Poles and Turks. So democracy can at most be a necessary and sufficient condition for tolerance on the state level, but it has little effect on what citizens feel deep in their hearts. I think that knowledge of the Holocaust should above all serve to soften those hearts.

Can tolerance toward a former foe be learned? And can knowledge about genocide be helpful in this? The path to tolerance, and further to reconciliation and forgiveness between former enemies, no doubt leads through knowledge of the Holocaust. Knowledge of the singular explosion of evil that occurred in Europe in the fifth decade of the last century. That knowledge should teach sensitivity to the suffering of others; it should compel an ethical examination, and reflection on human nature and the mechanisms of conflict. I do not think, however, that harmony and peace will prevail as this knowledge is spread among nations, ethnic groups, or individuals. In other words, I do not think that disseminating knowledge about the Holocaust will eliminate anti-Semitism!

If it is to be reduced in the future, something more is needed. Knowledge of the Holocaust must become one element of a broader education grounded in an interdisciplinary context of historical knowledge, psychological techniques of conflict resolution, sociological knowledge about stereotypes, etc.

Here I shall use an example from personal experience I have quoted often: "I know that the Jews don't drink blood, but a drop of Christian blood for the matzo is always needed." Such a thought occurred to an older gentleman during the discussion after a lecture by Rabbi Jules

Harlow at the Institute for Jewish-Christian Dialogue of the Catholic Theological Academy in Warsaw in the spring of 1996.[14] A month earlier, at a conference on relations between Jews and Christians organized by the Polish Institute in Stockholm, Rabbi Harlow had declared, "Poland is the last place on earth my wife and I would want to visit."[15] When he learned that in 1944 my father was shot by the Germans in the Warsaw Uprising, he said, "For the first time I see Poles as victims."

No doubt both the rabbi and the Christian participant in the dialogue encounter had sufficient knowledge of the Holocaust; despite this, stereotypes did their thinking for them, stereotypes sprung from the blank spots in their historical knowledge. In this case, it was more a lack of general knowledge that determined the intolerance and enmity, rather than ignorance of the Holocaust. The ritual murder accusation, tragic in its results for the Jews, stands in contradiction to elementary knowledge of Judaism, in which blood is a major taboo. In turn, not seeing Poles as victims of the Second World War results from a lack of elementary historical knowledge of that war. (It is unnecessary to add that in Poland the numbers of victims among Jews and Poles were similar – except that about 10% of the Poles lost their lives, while less than 10% of the Jews survived. Those proportions are very hard to grasp rationally.)

On the other hand, one should not underestimate the importance of knowledge about the Holocaust. Demythologized knowledge of the Holocaust is particularly important to us Poles. Jan T. Gross, the author of *Neighbors*, wrote, "Will acceptance of responsibility for odious deeds perpetrated during World War II – on top of a deeply ingrained, and

---

[14] Presently named Cardinal Stefan Wyszyński University.

[15] After the Stockholm conference, Rabbi Jules Harlow changed his negative stance and since then he has visited Poland many times, becoming engaged in Polish-Jewish reconciliation. He has also co-authored a Polish-Swedish multicultural program on the Holocaust and modern forms of religious and ethnic prejudice.

well-deserved, sense of victimization suffered at the time – come easily and naturally to the Polish public?"[16]

In Polish-Jewish relations, dissemination of knowledge about the Holocaust could make some Jews stop seeing Poles as the main perpetrators, and make Poles finally perceive the sufferings of their closest neighbors and take to heart the shameful truth – that sometimes not Germans but we Poles were the cause of it. This will only happen if both peoples, joined by so many bonds in the past, stop concentrating exclusively on their own pain and become capable of understanding the pain of the other party. "How can you be my friend," wondered a certain *tzaddik*, "when you don't even know what pains me?" Let's not fool ourselves, however – forget about adults. Polish-Jewish reconciliation will take place through the efforts of the third post-Holocaust generation. So let us teach all of it to our children from the start.

---

[16] J.T. Gross, *Neighbors: The Destruction of the Jewish Community in Jedwabne*, Princeton 2001, p. 145.

Stanisław Krajewski

Teach Everywhere, and Especially in Poland!

There are universal reasons, European and Christian reasons, and specifically Polish reasons. Do the universal ones apply to everyone? It would be hard to argue that in India or Japan they should teach about the Holocaust of Jews somewhere in Europe. There have been so many massacres and genocides across the span of history, in every corner of the globe. They should teach about the ones that affect them directly. And yet, in Japan there is interest in the Shoah! They come to Auschwitz. They sense the presence of evil there. Auschwitz has become a symbol clear to the whole world, probably to some extent because Western culture is omnipresent, and in this culture, much intellectual and emotional energy has been devoted to the problem of the Holocaust. Why? What makes this genocide different from others?

One way of answering is to point out the means used by Nazi Germany: true factories of death were organized. The best organizers and modern knowledge were employed to make the assembly-line proceed with the greatest efficiency. The product was death. The Holocaust of the Jews thus becomes a warning: this is what technological development without moral progress can lead to. (Another example even better illustrates the problem of misguided scientific advance – the atom bomb.) The second answer to the question of the uniqueness of the Holocaust points to the extent of the enterprise. The Germans wanted to eliminate all Jews from the face of the earth. In one country after another they introduced a system that would enable the capture of every Jew, old people and babies as well. War aims were not the point. It is known that sometimes the killing of Jews interfered with the achievement of war aims because, for example, it required the use of means of transport that could have been of use to the soldiers. This becomes understandable when we consider the third answer to the question of uniqueness: the goal was to cleanse the world. Murdering Jews was not pleasant. It was understood, however, to be an essential step in the achievement of a grand ideological vision: rule by a better race and the removal of the personification of evil – the Jews, according to Hitler – from humanity. These circumstances are worth studying, because they say something important about our civilization. They also point to the fourth answer: it was not about just anyone, but about the Jews.

In Europe and North America, and also in other countries whose culture has European roots, the Holocaust must be seen as the culmination of many centuries of anti-Semitism. It did not have to happen, but the ground prepared by Christianity enabled the growth of murderous anti-Semitism. The ground was the Christian vision of Jews as a nation of Christ-killers and as a people hardened in their rejection of the truth taught by the Church and therefore deserving of humiliation and persecution. This led to outright demonization of the Jews. And isn't it right to get rid of the devil? When it was realized in the West that "ordinary" anti-Semitism could turn into a campaign to systematically murder every Jew within reach, in the center of Christian Europe, it brought shock. Particularly when it became clear that no few people actively or passively supported the Holocaust, and that those who opposed it saw that as a priority only rarely. This shock led to a profound revaluation of the Church's attitude toward the Jews and the Jewish religion. It became the basis for a historically new phenomenon: Christian-Jewish dialogue conducted on the basis of partnership. This dialogue is going forward, though many Christians and Jews still see no sense in partnering with the misguided other side.

The Holocaust also fundamentally affected the attitudes of Jews. It sparked determination to achieve Jewish sovereignty in the Land of Israel. And what happens there impacts the world. Jerusalem is important to Christians and also to Muslims. Its current fate cannot be understood without some knowledge of the Holocaust, which left a deep, unhealed wound. More generally, the Jews played a special role in the history of Christianity. Judaism is the root. Thus, the attitude to the Jews is a component of the attitude toward one's own roots. The majority of European Jews were murdered. If the war had gone differently, there would be no Jews now – the children would have murdered the mother. That is why the Jewish tragedy is a special challenge for the West.

Poland is part of Europe and the Christian world, so all the above arguments should apply. At the same time, in Poland there was no shock comparable with the one in the West. That is why one of the most lethal slanders in history – accusing the Jews of ritual murder – is dying a harder death in Poland than in the West. A mural depicting this accusation in the Sandomierz Cathedral still has no plaque informing viewers that it does not reflect the truth. After the war, Poles lamented the harm and losses inflicted on them. The Polish sense of being victims *par excellence*, that no one could have suffered more than they had, demanded that the Jewish Holocaust be spoken of as a part, a small part at that, of Polish losses. At the Auschwitz site, for years no one mentioned that the great majority of the victims were Jews. It is worth teaching Polish youth about the Holocaust if only to debunk that image.

There are many more of these specifically Polish circumstances. Ninety percent of the Polish Jews perished. This changed Poland's human and social landscape. Moreover, it was in Poland that the death factories operated. Is it possible not to teach about what happened right here so recently? It is a part of Polish history. The Holocaust cannot be compared to any tragedy within reach of the collective memory. Whole families perished, and no one remained even to remember them, let alone bury them. All of Polish society of the day was witness to those events. That role of witness to the tragedy is not without psychological consequences. As yet there has been no deeper examination of them. Some literary and cinematic works take up the problem. The psychological consequences cannot be understood without knowledge of the realities. By not teaching about the Holocaust we make it impossible to understand some of the poems of Czesław Miłosz, Wisława Szymborska, Krzysztof Baczyński or Jerzy Ficowski.

Poles were not only witnesses of the Holocaust. There were also those who cooperated in it. Although the main and the ultimate perpetrators were Germans, the participation of Poles was not always the result of compulsion by the occupier, not always the act of degenerate people from the fringes of society. The murder of Jews in Jedwabne in July 1941 did not become the subject of public discussion until 2000. For decades it was a taboo topic. It was not spoken of publicly although everyone in the town knew about it. Jedwabne was not the only one. The extent of the taboo is still unknown, but it is clear that there is something to teach.

Poles are justly proud of the number of Polish "Righteous Among the Nations" honored in Israel for aiding Jews during the war. I too think that they deserve to be seen as Poland's best representatives. However, their deeds can be appreciated only when the context of their actions is taught, showing why it required heroism. And the reason was not only the ruthlessness of the German occupiers, but also the frequent ill will of their Polish neighbors. Moreover, one outcome of the murder of Jews was the appropriation of their homes and much property by the neighbors. The effect of this on Poland then – and Poland now, when reprivatization has become a subject of debate – is little recognized.[17] To teach all this is to introduce students to a difficult but necessary truth about life. Finally, in Poland as in Israel and everywhere else, it is necessary to have the kind of education that shows how teaching contempt can lead to killing. The Shoah provides an object lesson.

---

[17] The term "reprivatization" is used in Poland to refer to restitution of property to its original owners, not to privatization of state-owned companies.

Stanisław Obirek SJ

The Long Shadow of Bełżec

Today one cannot write or speak about the Holocaust in Poland without including what happened in Jedwabne on July 10, 1941. Leaving the details to be established by historians, I would like to recall a statement by Rabbi Jacob Baker, who is from Jedwabne. Asked whether he expected apologies from Poles, he said this:

> I expect sincere contrition. That would be the best apology, and the best way to extend the hand of reconciliation to Jews. Many of them, especially in Israel, do remember Poland, and have good memories of it. Maybe it will surprise you, but Jews are grateful to Poland that for a thousand years it was their home, it gave them shelter, and our culture flourished most beautifully here. What a beautiful country, Poland! How beautiful nature is there. I remember Jedwabne, what a pretty place. I remember Jedwabne. I could have said, "to hell with the Poles, may they disappear," but believe me, I don't feel that way. Jews don't feel that way. We do not have revenge on our minds. Only God has the right to take vengeance. We would only want the murderers to be punished if some of them are still alive. Them, yes, because they deserve punishment. But ordinary Poles, the ordinary residents of Jedwabne? They were decent. We were good neighbors, friends.

In this same interview by Krzysztof Darewicz of New York for *Rzeczpospolita* newspaper, he added, "I believe that although there no longer are Jews in Poland, our friendship cannot be forgotten. It has to be maintained and strengthened, with good will shown on both sides. I am convinced that this is possible, even knowing what happened in Jedwabne."

Rabbi Baker was born in 1914, so he is a wise elder. I have met many such people, older even, but more younger ones – both Christians and Jews. I am convinced that friendship between Christians and Jews is not only possible but is already a fact. It does not have to be proposed or appealed to; it needs to be described and spoken of as much as possible. It is in speaking of such friendships that I see the only possibility of meaningfully (that is, in a way that enables us to uncover the meaning hidden in the tragedy of the Holocaust) talking about what happened to humanity during the Second World War. Because the Holocaust is not only the tragedy of the Jewish people; it is the tragedy of all of us, and we all are responsible for it.

I want to tell about my attempt (which has barely begun) to understand the Holocaust. It is marked by the place where I was born, in Tomaszów Lubelski, and the place where I grew up, in Narol. Both towns are next to Bełżec, one of the locations of the German death camps for Jews, in which, in less than a year (from February to November 1942), 600,000 European Jews were savagely murdered along with 1,500 Polish Christians who had tried to help their Jewish neighbors survive.[18] I have visited the Bełżec camp many times, first as a child not completely realizing what I was seeing, and later after becoming a priest. I have looked at the place through the eyes of my guests. Every visit has deepened my awareness that we, Christians and Jews, are the ones who must remember the victims. I can still see before me the deeply moved reaction of my

---

[18] Originally, the plaque commemorating the death of 600,000 Jews at Bełżec also had a reference to 1,500 non-Jewish Poles killed there for having aided Jews, but in the absence of written proof it was removed. In my opinion there is no reason to eradicate the traces of their existence. New research, I hope, will justify the original inscription. Abraham Cykiert and Henryk Luft, Jews mentioned in this essay, confirmed me in this belief.

friend Abraham Cykiert from far-off Melbourne. That same evening, after returning to Cracow, he wrote a stirring essay.[19] Abraham had experienced the Łódź ghetto and the hell of Auschwitz. Perhaps that is why he heard the voices of the Bełżec victims so clearly, but thanks to his sensitivity we too can hear those voices.

Henryk Luft of Israel, who is among the few fortunate ones who managed to escape from there, speaks of it differently. He tells his story without bitterness. What he has preserved is a sense of gratitude:

> We arrived from Lwów in the morning. I managed to slip out of the rail car, and two other boys with me. They ran in one direction and were shot on the spot. I made it. I knocked on a window. An older woman opened it for me, and gave me bread and warm milk. She showed how to get to Rawa Ruska – we had a relative there who was a pharmacist. Along the way I met a peasant with a wagon. When I asked how far it was to Rawa, he said "Get in." I awoke next to those same railroad tracks in Bełżec. He just said to get out of the wagon and left. By some miracle a woman with two milk cans was approaching. I grabbed one and went along. When the Ukrainian policemen asked, she answered, "He's ours." That saved me. I could talk about it for a long time. But why return to it.

Henryk returned to Bełżec and looked for the home that had saved his life, but there everything had changed. There are more stories like that. They should be recalled and recounted.

I return to Bełżec very willingly. I walk around that forgotten cemetery of European Jews. I think of those 1,500 Christians who were murdered together with the 600,000 Jews. I think of Abraham Cykiert, of Henryk Luft, of those who helped and whom no one remembers. How to join the memory of Bełżec, of the Jews of Tomaszów and Narol, with the

---

[19] A. Cykiert, "Milczenie Bełżca," *Więź* 2001, no. 4, pp. 59–62.

collective memory of my native region? I think, and cannot think of anything. Perhaps such an initiative as the publication of this little book is an answer of a kind? Perhaps. I would like to think so, and that is why I have written these few lines about the long shadow of Bełżec.

Tanna Jakubowicz-Mount

In a Spirit of Reconciliation

What's the purpose of human evolution?
Some think we are here to gain divine
knowledge of how to combine opposites
and reconcile contradictions.
David Lynch

I am deeply convinced that the spirit of the new times is a spirit of reconciliation. Reconciliation of man with the world, people with people, man
with himself. We seem to be beginning to understand that it makes no
sense to direct human energy against life. But the road to making this
reconciliation a reality is long. If we do not want to pass a legacy of violence to our children, we have to heal evil at its root, and this means to
shed light on the dark side of our mentality. If the Holocaust is to be taught
about, it means not only revealing the truth about the past, but showing
how the same mechanisms operate in the world here and now, in different
societies and in man himself.

The Holocaust – still-living history

The question of why intolerance, xenophobia, nationalism, fascism and
fundamentalism raise their heads not only in Poland but also in many places
around the world calls for deep reflection. I am not alone in my conviction
that we are living in a time of identity crisis. Humanity at the turn of the

century, a time of transformation, feels threatened by the world's inconstancy and unpredictability, and fears the disappearance of boundaries, the loss of individuality. Spiritual teachers from different traditions say that the most visible signs of a time of change are chaos, a spiritual vacuum, and fear of the unknown. When the ground shifts under our feet, we cling tightly to a given identity and affiliation: national, political or religious. I am a Pole, a Catholic, a Jew, a German. Fear of the unknown world finds its outlet in fear and hatred of "strangers." Nationalism and fascism draw new energy in this way, providing an outward sense of identity and power. The longing for an ordered, divided-up world seems to me to be the greatest danger, because that image of a world stamped with divisions, that "I – Not I" opposition, is the source of fear, enmity, suffering and violence. Thus it seems to me all the more urgent to convey the experience of and knowledge about the Holocaust to young people. We have two paths to choose from: either domination by the old order based on human ignorance and fear, or the creation of a new model of coexistence on the basis of a clear mind, an open heart, and empathy.

A community of suffering

I agree with Jan Gross, who said that dealing with the legacy of the Holocaust demands from us spiritual evolution and transformation above all. What does that mean? I shall start with my own example as an illustration of inner work, which can be difficult but extraordinarily helpful. The question of how to encounter the stranger in oneself and in other people enters not only into my work with people but also deeply into my spiritual life and practice. Every November for the last five years I have sat to meditate on the ramp in Birkenau, where trains from all over Europe reached their final end. Together with me sit a huge international group of people who have come from around the world – Jews, Germans, French, Japanese, Poles and other people of different nationalities, religions, denominations and skin colors. This takes place within a program of retreats run by the Zen Peacemaker Order, an interfaith organization founded by the Buddhist teacher Bernie Glassman.

The purpose of this meditation is to bear witness to what we apprehend in experiencing our presence at that place, in the face of the horrible crimes that were committed there. First I felt shock, realizing the extraordinary precision with which the machinery of death had been organized. I felt enormous hatred for the perpetrators who had granted themselves the right to be masters of life and death and to destroy millions of human beings. Later I went deeper into the process of identifying with the many people from my family who perished in Auschwitz. I wanted to unite with them in their suffering, to feel with my whole self their despair, their terror in the face of death, of being torn away from everything... In the crematorium, along with others in the circle I recited their names aloud.

When I went there the second time, I sensed that I could identify not only with the victims. I began to discover within myself that stranger, the perpetrator hiding in the shadow of my higher soul. My inner child emerged, who in her time had been left marked by the specters of the last war. So wounded and humiliated that she had dreamt of revenge, of taking vengeance against her persecutors, of inflicting pain and watching them suffer. Then a poem came...

> From a wounded child you can grow up to be a wounded tormentor
> Or a wounded healer.
> With the same hands, with that same energy
> You can kill or heal.
> Which do you choose?
> Do you who wound and kill see the people before you,
> Or phantoms spun from your pain, fear and humiliation.
> Do you prefer to shatter the mirror before you instead of seeing
> Your own shadow?

During our meetings in Auschwitz I saw children of the Holocaust and children of SS officers weep in each others' arms. After the "dark night of the soul," that generation is making a tremendous effort to sit together, to deeply feel the suffering of the other, and to join together in a heartfelt intention to leave mutual rancor behind, to forgive each other.

How to teach about the Holocaust in schools?

Now I shall try to generalize and objectivize this experience in order to formulate a sound program to convey knowledge of the Holocaust. It is not a matter of dividing the world into perpetrators and victims, of shooting at each other from behind the piles of corpses, because this can only fan hatred and vengefulness. The point is to expose the roots of evil and uncover the truth, because only what is exposed can be disarmed. I suggest, then, that a teaching program about the Shoah should include the following stages:

1. **Bearing witness to the truth** – bearing witness to the truth about our life and experience. This has a cleansing and healing effect. It would be good to invite witnesses, the people closest to direct experience of persecutions, or to offer diaries, memoirs, interviews, films with people who experienced the Holocaust directly, and taped interviews with victims.[20]

2. **Demonstrating the community of suffering** – conveying the message that there is no pain in the world that does not affect us. Genocide is the shared pain of all humanity, and it demands a global solution. Victim and perpetrator often spring from the very same root – suffering, despair and humiliation.

---

[20] Many resources can be found at www.vhf.org (Survivors of the Shoah. Visual History Foundation).

3. **Meeting the stranger in ourselves and others** – exposing, through workshop activity, the mechanism of projection, to show how we fear meeting our own dark side, how unrecognized aspects of ourselves – difficult, painful, dark and stigmatized aspects – are projected onto the world, and how in this way we create our enemies and turn our aggression toward others, making them victims of our aversion to our own selves. In this way we add to the world's suffering. The so-called stranger reveals our unwanted side to us. I suggest the workshop which for some time I have been conducting during international "Meeting the Stranger" gatherings. The point of this work is to identify, understand, accept and reconcile conflicted parts of ourselves. The person who accepts himself entirely does not cast a shadow upon the world.

4. **Working on the mechanism of frustration and deprivation** – showing the ways in which socially frustrated people look for inferiors in order to release their anger at the world.

5. **Working on myths, stereotypes and prejudices** – examining the myths and stereotypes about different nationalities involved in conflict, and how to neutralize them.

6. **Sensitizing children and youth** – fostering their sensitivity to values such as the preciousness of human life and life in general, their tolerance toward the differentness of other people, their appreciation of all people's fundamental right to a free, decent and fulfilled life, their capacity for empathy with the suffering, and their sense of mutual dependence and connection with all living beings.

7. **Showing the common root of all religions and spiritual traditions** – conveying the kind of idea I communicated to His Holiness the Dalai Lama during his visit to Poland: "I believe that humanity is like one huge, beautiful, strong tree whose roots draw from the common soil which is the ground of the different cultures and spiritual tradi-

tions. The trunk is shared, and the crown with its thousands of branches and millions of leaves mirrors our sacred differences and sacred community. We should create a Council of the World's Elders, consisting of the wise mentors from the different traditions, in order to cultivate our Tree of Life together."

I think that already, very gradually, our evolution from *homo tribus* to *homo holos* is proceeding. Tribal man sees the world as a battlefield, fights to hold on to territory and survive, and is motivated by fear of the stranger. Whole man has the capacity to unite with the whole community – human, planetary, and cosmic. I believe that the only place where this transformation from tribal to whole man can take place is the human heart. When enough of us learn how to make use of our natural ability to love and heal, how to rid ourselves of hatred and the desire to harm, when we replace the old model of perpetrator and victim with one based on love and partnership, we shall no longer pass a legacy of violence to new generations.

Stefan Wilkanowicz

Let's Try to Understand!

A few years ago, reflecting on the war in the Balkans, I came to the conclusion that no European should receive a high school diploma if he cannot sensibly answer three questions:

1. Why Auschwitz?
2. Why Kolyma?
3. Why Sarajevo?

If he does not answer, it means he does not understand basic historical facts, he may prove defenseless against new conflicts, and he may not understand the tragedies that have occurred on other continents (Cambodia, Rwanda) and for which Europe bears some responsibility.

In preparing a dossier on the subject of the anticulture of hatred and the culture of solidarity, centered mainly around the conflicts in the countries of former Yugoslavia, we observed that the methods of provoking aggression are similar or the same in all the mentioned instances.[21] They serve to awaken race, class and ethnic hatred. They can be employed in different circumstances and against various real enemies or others artificially created for one purpose or another. They are employed today and they will be employed in the future, so they need to be recognized, and we have to know how to prevent and counter them.

---

[21] The dossier was prepared for the EuroDialog Internet service, accessible through www.znak.com.pl/eurodialog

Though their propaganda methods are similar, each of these tragedies has its particular characteristics. The Shoah is distinctive not in terms
of the number of victims (class hatred has taken more of them) but in
terms of other circumstances. It was the first time it was decided to exterminate an entire people, including old people and children. Rational in-
dustrial methods were applied to the task, but at the same time the process
was lent a quasimystical quality; this mass murder was seen as an almost
redemptive duty to the German nation and to humanity, a kind of reverse
soteriology, salvation based purely on hatred. The rational fused with the
diabolical.

Every political, economic and psychological factor that led to or
facilitated the Holocaust can and must be studied. This is essential for the
prevention of similar tragedies. But it must be fully recognized that they
do not explain everything, that there is some mystery here, some depth of
evil which escapes us, and which demands some sort of spiritual response,
and not only the interventions of professional educators.

The same applies to Hitler and his devotees. One can fathom the
causes of his anti-Semitism, but it is hard to grasp his demonic character.
It is also hard to understand ultimately how he infected masses of people with that demonic virus, how ordinary, fairly decent people became
fanatic torturers without abandoning their nice bourgeois virtues.

All this presents educators with a mammoth task. How to convey it
all? How to communicate the uncommunicable? How to provide knowledge and a spiritual response?

Approaching these tasks realistically, first we have to supply book
knowledge, because most often it is lacking, and without it the rest is
impossible. This knowledge must be given not merely as something that
happened but as something that *can* happen. This seems shocking, but it is
not a psychological maneuver to shock young people. It has to be known
that man is capable of great evil, and young people do know this. They

also know that in our communities there are poisons that lead to hatred and violence. "Hate is now in style," wrote a high school student answering a "youth and violence" survey. Others are pessimistic; they feel powerless against evil. There are also those who want to combat it, who seek ways of acting against it. They can be the best teachers of their peers. Often they are the ones who most deeply feel the tragedy of the Shoah and other calamities of our age, and they have a better understanding of their peers. So let us make them full partners in meeting the joint responsibility to learn about that tragedy and to draw conclusions from it.

Let us beware of isolating the Shoah from other tragedies, however, because we have to build broad solidarity against contempt, hatred and violence – solidarity among people who feel close to other catastrophes of humanity, as well as those who feel a particular link with the tragedy of the Holocaust.

Robert Szuchta

Against Silence and Indifference
Why I teach about the Holocaust – reflections of a teacher

The road to Auschwitz was paved
with the stones of indifference.

I was born in Warsaw and live there. Before the Second World War it had one of the largest Jewish communities in the world. The Jewish citizens of my town had their streets and homes here, their shops and theaters, businesses, schools and synagogues. Here they published many periodicals and books, and studied the holy books of Judaism. They dreamed of building a Jewish state in Palestine, but they also considered how to achieve harmonious coexistence with the Poles in a shared home, Poland. Their culture radiated to the whole world and enriched Poland's culture. As a result of the Holocaust – the planned, institutionalized, organized and systematically implemented extermination of six million children, women and men – this world ceased to exist. The single and sufficient reason for their killing was that they were born Jews.

Many years after these events, as a pupil in a Polish school, I searched in vain in the history textbooks for information on how the Polish Jews lived and how they perished. From I.B. Singer's writings I learned that the Poles and the Jews had lived next to but not with each other for eight hundred years. I found out how difficult it is to work the history of the Jews and their Holocaust into the mainstream of Polish history. On the occasion of observances commemorating the last war, the martyrdom and heroism of the Polish nation were placed in the foreground until only recently. Schools and scout troops were named after Polish war heroes. In memoirs there was no room for my city's Jewish residents, who in 1942 went to the Umschlagplatz from where they took their last journey in cattle cars to death in the gas chambers and crematoria of Treblinka. Nor was there room for the heroic handful of Jewish youth who in the spring of 1943 launched an uprising in the Warsaw ghetto. Today, as a teacher, I cannot fail to teach about the history and culture of the Polish Jews. They who died in an inhuman manner cry out to us: "Remember, do not forget, speak of us to the next generations." I keep hearing that voice. It calls to me from the cobbles of Warsaw's streets, from the Umschlagplatz, from the ruins of the gas chambers in Auschwitz-Birkenau, and from the burning barn in Jedwabne. I cannot remain indifferent to that cry. Who is to speak of this? Those who could do so have passed on.

Years ago, Theodor Adorno stated that the task of teaching after Auschwitz is to oppose barbarity. According to the philosopher, the Holocaust was barbarity, and the frightening thing is that barbarity remains a possibility so long as conditions permitting its return exist. The modern history of Europe confirms those fears. Srebrenica, Kosovo, Rwanda and many other places in the world do not allow us to forget the atrocities of sixty years ago. The link between contemporary genocide and the Holocaust compels me to consider what I should do so that my students know and try to understand what took place, so that they can counteract the barbarity Adorno warned against.

I teach about the Holocaust because in conveying knowledge about the history of Poland I must not forget that Jews lived among us for hundreds of years and created their own original culture, which enriched Polish culture. After all, it is difficult to explain Poland's history without discussing the place and role of Jews in it. If I overlook this part of Polish history, the students will receive fragmentary, incomplete knowledge, and this means that the picture of the past will be false. The history of Poland is the story of a multiethnic state and society, the achievement of the many peoples inhabiting Polish soil, including Jews. That world ceased to exist more than sixty years ago. It was ended in such a dramatic way by the Holocaust.

I teach about the Holocaust because it occurred on Polish soil, against the will of Poles but in their presence. This prompts the question of the variety of attitudes toward the Holocaust. How did Poles comport themselves in the face of the Holocaust of their Jewish fellow citizens and neighbors? How did other communities of Europe and the world behave? What was known? What was done? Although this problem has been raised in the literature many times and continues to be raised, it still awaits an unequivocal appraisal. However, this does not release me as a teacher from considering and discussing this difficult – and for many, painful – question with my students.

I teach about the Holocaust because it is a unique event in modern history. I would like my students to understand that uniqueness, to be able to evaluate it independently, to be able to tell the difference between genocidal acts such as pogroms, the genocide of the Thirty Years' War period (1618–1648), the Armenian genocide in 1915, the extermination of Polish people in the years of World War II, the Stalinist crimes symbolized by *The Gulag Archipelago*, or the ethnic cleansing in former Yugoslavia, Rwanda and Kosovo. That will allow them to understand the scale and character of the particular instances of genocide that have befallen humanity over the span of history, and to perceive the uniqueness of the Holocaust against that background.

The uniqueness of the Holocaust is tied to a further argument for including it in history classes in school. Rabbi Byron L. Sherman, who has devoted 30 years to teaching about this event, states that it is a paradigmatic event of modern history. He compares the Holocaust to an earthquake, and sees it as the first and the strongest quake, which is followed by aftershocks. The results of the Holocaust are felt to this day, and the aftershocks are the terrorist acts, ethnic cleansing and mass murders of populations committed in different corners of the world. The reflection that accompanies teaching about this event creates sensitivity to those aftershocks. It makes us ask ourselves: what can we do so that they never recur? The question, after all, is not pointless.

I teach about the Holocaust so that my students will remember what happened, so they will not be silent in the face of the evil which unfortunately is present in our lives. It is said that sin begins with a word, but sin also begins with the silence that becomes assent and which can be tantamount to participation. Protesting against the unfolding Holocaust of the Jews, in 1942 Zofia Kossak-Szczucka wrote:

> The world watches these crimes, more terrible than anything history has seen – and is mute. The slaughter of millions of defenseless people is taking place amidst a general, sinister silence.... This silence cannot be tolerated. Whatever its motives, it is depraved. Whoever is mute in the face of murder becomes the murderer's accomplice. Whoever does not condemn it permits it.[22]

I believe that these words are still relevant today. The truth that the writer has conveyed to us must be borne in mind if we want the evil never to be repeated again. I want to pass this truth to my students.

Finally, the most obvious reason I teach about the Holocaust is that it is an element not only of the Jews' history but of world history and Poland's history. Thus it should be a subject of teaching in Polish schools. I would like all graduating students to have a basic knowledge of as many

---

[22] "Protest – odezwa conspiracyjnego Frontu Odrodzenia Polski," in A.K. Kunert, *Polacy – Żydzi. 1939–1945. Wybór źródeł*, Warsaw 2001, p. 213.

issues as possible, and to understand them, because they are entering adult life supplied with a general education.

For me the Holocaust is an event without precedent in modern world history. In teaching about it I am making my students aware of the dangers inherent in intolerance, nationalism, xenophobia or totalitarianism. It seems to me that the best way to do this is not merely to provide students with the basic facts of the Holocaust but to reveal and analyze the mechanisms that allowed it. I am convinced that if we want to mold an open, tolerant person who is sensitive to suffering and respects the life and dignity of his fellow man, we should provide solid knowledge of a time when people were barbarously deprived of dignity and life. Teaching about the Holocaust is not an easy task, but it is worth taking the trouble, in the hope that we will at least slightly change ourselves, others, and the world, which will become less brutal and more bearable. I have faith in this.

Sergiusz Kowalski

It's Obvious

Why teach about the Holocaust? And why not? It happened on Polish soil, after all, and not all that long ago, in my parents' generation. We don't ask whether to teach – and we do teach – about things from much earlier times, good and bad. About the dynasties of Polish kings, their feats and reverses, the splitting of Poland into duchies in 1138, the election of kings by the nobility, the Four-Years' Sejm, the Confederation of Bar and the Confederation of Targowice, the partitions, uprisings, and grass-roots reform movements under foreign occupation. About the recovery of independence, the death of President Narutowicz, and Piłsudski's May 1926 coup. About the Second World War, about the struggle and suffering of the Polish nation.

Why, then, not teach about the Holocaust, which engulfed millions of Poland's Jewish citizens and Jews from all over Europe who were transported and methodically murdered in Auschwitz, Birkenau, Treblinka, Bełżec and Sobibór. Is that less important? It is not those who say "teach it" who should explain their view, but those who still keep asking "just why, exactly." That is basically the most important reason: it has to be taught, simply because it took place. Because it is a part – and what an important part – of modern Polish history, regardless of the fact that the death camps were organized by Germans, German Nazis. They organized them here, in Poland, and put to death millions of Jews in them, a large part of them Polish citizens. Thus the subject would be unavoidable even if the teaching of history and literature were to be maintained in its obsolete, Polonocentric form, that is, with Poland's history purged of information about the spiritual and material culture of the Jews, Germans, Italians, Dutch, French and many others who made outstanding contributions.

Another question can be put, however. Not "why," because that is completely obvious, but "what for," "for what purpose." Such a purpose would be to restore accuracy to history, to make essential corrections, and especially to fill in the huge gaps left from communist teaching. There are many such things which must be taught because they have never been taught up to now. When it comes to the Jews, in the schools of the Polish People's Republic one could learn in history classes that in Auschwitz the Nazis murdered all the peoples of Europe according to an alphabetical list beginning with Albanians and Austrians and ending with Jews.[23] Yes, also Jews; but Jews were the ones in the huge majority, and this was not mentioned – those Austrians, French, Hungarians and even Germans murdered as Jews. Who in those schools had an opportunity to learn anything at all about "the blackmailing of hidden Jews, the Polish police working for the occupier, the Baudienst formations in which Polish youth served, the Warsaw pogrom of Easter 1940, priests handing over Jews after hearing confession ... of Jedwabne and Radziłów, of the innocent custom of 'burning Judas' during the war ... of the glasses of water sold for gold coins to the Jews who were crammed into the death trains. Or about the 'rail actions' of 1945 in which National Armed Forces partisans pulled out of trains and shot about 200 repatriated Jews being resettled from the east ... about the postwar killings of Jews returning home from exile, about the Kielce and Cracow pogroms, and the hundreds of other unidentified denunciations of wartime and postwar reality."[24]

---

[23] In Polish the word for "Jew" begins with the letter "Ż."

[24] J. Tokarska-Bakir, "Obsesja niewinności," *Gazeta Wyborcza*, January 13–14, 2001, pp. 22–23, published as part of the discussion of Jedwabne.

In communist times, school teaching, including history teaching, was not pure Marxist propaganda. True, it did ignore facts inconvenient to the regime, for example Stalin's murder of the majority of the Polish Communist Party's leaders, but it also ignored other facts troubling to the historical image of Poland as undeviatingly tolerant, unstained by collaboration, fighting "for our freedom and yours," pure, noble and beautiful, if one ignores the few representatives of the "age-old renegade camp of backwardness, obscurantism and reaction." Let's note that all the intricate historical meanders were supposed to have led, by the inevitable logic of history, toward the reality of People's Poland, the land of fulfilled dreams. The omissions and distortions were often deliberate, not motivated by propaganda considerations, because among those who transmitted the vision of history in the days of the Polish People's Republic there were also nationalists among the communists – the precursors, architects and creators of the infamous anti-Semitic campaign of 1968. Some of them, the likes of Leszek Andrzej Szcześniak, to this day are writing history textbooks, improved but kept in that same tone, and recommended by the Ministry of Education despite the protests of the leading experts and intellectuals.

Not only the faction around Central Committee member Mieczysław Moczar, but other champions of wrongheaded patriotism as well, preferred not to let young people know about the darker chapters of Polish history, and the flaws in Polish tolerance. Not until recently have many articles in the press (and not yet in textbooks) treated Polish-Jewish subjects without the customary hackneyed falsehoods and insinuations. Rev. Stanisław Musiał SJ, for example, writes candidly and acidly:

> For at least three centuries the Church in Poland tolerated, supported, and usually initiated trials against Jews about so-called ritual murder, and this against the teaching of the popes. As the result of more than a hundred trials

in this matter, many hundreds of people suffered death, preceded by cruel tortures – not to mention the constant fear in which the Jewish communities lived, because every chance discovery of a child's corpse could be used against them. The Church in Poland was loath to condemn humiliating mistreatment of Jews, especially during Christian holidays, and did nothing against these practices. Let a quotation serve as an example, from the 1618 work *Mirror of the Polish Crown. The serious harm and great trouble it suffers from the Jews,* written by Rev. Sebastian Miczyński: "There is no one to humble the Jew, and that hallowed and praiseworthy custom has disappeared, when, seeing a Jew in town on a holy day, the boys and innocent children would chase him away with stones and mud, and pull him by the beard, avenging the Lord's suffering."[25] The Church in Poland did not defend the good name of Jews and took no action against the flood of vulgar anti-Semitic publications, beginning with a collection of extraordinary slanders against the Jews in the notorious book *The Jews' Animosity Toward God* by Rev. Gaudencjusz Pikulski from the mid 18th century,[26] and ending in the third-rate journalism practiced by priests in the interwar period. These are some of the sins of the Church in Poland as an institution, for which apologies to the Jews should be made.[27]

Let us add that even today the Bishop of Sandomierz has not yet ordered removed, or even appropriately labeled, the picture of ritual murder publicly exhibited in the church there, an example of the early iconography of accusations drastically at odds with the entire spirit and letter of Judaism.

Others are writing, reconstructing the true picture, far from the stereotyped ideal, of how Polish-Jewish relations were:

[25] S. Myczyński, *Zwierciadło Korony Polskiej, urazy ciężkie utrapienie wielkie, które ponosi od Żydów wyrażaiące synom Koronnym na Seym walny w roku pańskim 1616 przez...*, Kraków 1616.

[26] G. Pikulski, *Złość żydowska preciwko Bogu y bliźniemu prawdzie y sumieniu na obiaznienie Talmudystów*, Lwów 1758.

[27] S. Musiał SJ, "Prosimy, pomóżcie nam być lepszymi," *Gazeta Wyborcza*, May 21, 2001, pp. 24–25.

[Niemcewicz] believed in the "Talmudic poison" eating at the Jews' viscera – and was aghast.[28]

Duke Adam Czartoryski along with the Reform Committee declared in 1816 that the Jews could not yet be granted civil rights, since first they had to be "improved," that is, freed of the "ignorance, superstitions and moral corruption we see in the Jewish masses."[29]

She graduated high school very young, and right away to Liege to study medicine! Because in Warsaw at that time, especially in that faculty, there was not merely a *numerus clausus* for Jews, but in practice a *numerus nullus*. "Those were the worst times, you know, the bench ghetto, when Jewish students had to stand during the lectures. Professor Kotarbiński also used to stand then, but Tatarkiewicz sat," she adds as if embarrassed. "But I explain the Polish anti-Semitism of those days with poverty," she quickly concludes.[30]

For now at least, the collective memory is being reconstructed, the labor of committed essayists and journalists. Work on the canon of school education – and catechesis – is in its infancy. True, textbooks on the Holocaust are appearing, by Robert Szuchta and Piotr Trojański among others, but thoroughgoing change awaits a teaching methodology for – and a general willingness on the part of – the ordinary teachers of history and literature all over Poland who do not know the subject. The point is not to humiliate the Poles, to suddenly transform them from victims and heroes into a nation of blackmailers and torturers. That would be an equally false reversal of the stereotype. The point is for teachers and students in free Poland to recognize themselves as a more ordinary society – sometimes heroic, sometimes ignoble – like every other sensible nation.

---

[28] M. Janion, *Do Europy tak, ale razem z naszymi umarłymi*, Warsaw 2000, p. 123. Julian Ursyn Niemcewicz was a writer, politician, and hero of Poland's independence movement; he coauthored Poland's May 3rd Constitution of 1791.

[29] Ibidem, p. 104.

[30] E. Berberyusz, "Rzeczy śmieszne," *Rzeczpospolita*, April 11, 1998. Tadeusz Kotarbiński and Władysław Tatarkiewicz were eminent philosophers who taught at the University of Warsaw during the period in question.

Olga Goldberg-Mulkiewicz

The Holocaust
and the Folk Stereotype of the Jew

You have no little Jewish towns in Poland, none anymore.
In the windows of Hrubieszów, Karczew, Brody, Falenica,
there are no lighted candles, pointless to search for...
Elegy for the Shtetls

... thus wrote Antoni Słonimski in 1950, recalling a world that had ceased to be. At the time the poem appeared, however, that world did exist in memoirs and in people's memories. It was easy to find there. Today in seeking the Jewish world we often resort to what tradition tells us on the subject. Not to examine the concept of tradition in depth, I shall restrict myself to highlighting two of its basic features: it conveys the past to us selectively, and it perpetuates stereotypes that came into being at some earlier time. And we know, after all, that Polish society's centuries of living next to Jewish populations dwelling in tightly knit groups in towns and villages had to lead to the creation of the stereotype of the Jew, and then to its perpetuation in many elements of traditional folk culture. This stereotype emerged when the two cultures coexisted on the same land, and the basis for its creation was the differentness expressed in language, religion, ceremonies, dress, and so many other generally known features. The stereotype of the Jew appeared in the tradition of rural Poland next to the rest of the "others" such as the German, Hungarian, Gypsy or chimney sweep. He was encountered much more often, however, and was much richer in terms of both exterior attributes and the functions performed. Important to our considerations are the following questions, then: where should we look today for a traditional source conveying the figure of the Jew, what does that figure look like, and what are its fundamental features?

The frequency of occurrence of the stereotype of the Jew in the tradition of the Polish village or small town was largely associated with the variety of roles he played. We see this dichotomy clearly in Christmas plays or caroling customs featuring the figure of King Herod. Both of these customs have lost their currency, but they persist and form part of the array of spectacles performed not only locally but also in all kinds of competitions for folk ensembles. Today we also find the traditional figure of the Jew above all in souvenir figurines and trinkets intended mainly for tourists visiting Poland. Thus it seems important to trace, at least in a few examples, the diversity of the stereotype of the Jew as it is communicated nowadays.

We see this diversity most accurately in examining the role of the Jew in folk Christmas plays. Herod, the image of absolute evil – the Jewish king issuing an order to kill the innocent – is a Jew, but so is the rabbi, symbol of wisdom. The latter is summoned by Herod to pore through his books and interpret the future. In this same performance, a group of villagers on their way to Bethlehem call to their Jewish neighbor to come along with them to pay homage to the Christ child. Thus the village sees the neighbor as one of their own. During the intermissions of these plays a pair of "Jews" dance, sing and amuse the audience, taking on the role of jesters. Examining the role of the Jew in annual ceremonies related to the seasons, we see clearly that he is the protagonist of various scenes that are magical in nature, associated above all with the magic of the harvest cycle. He leads a goat, symbol of fertility, and when the goat falls he revives it;

this symbolizes the return of winter-dead nature to life. The Jew's costume is also associated with the magic of fertility: he is often hunchbacked, clothed in a sheepskin with the fleece worn outward, belted with a straw rope. And these, after all, are characteristics of a dichotomous figure. The variety of roles of the Jew is connected with the variety of costumes in which he appears, of course. The costume is as varied as the roles he plays. In contrast to the generally accepted conception, the Jew appearing in annual ceremonies very seldom appears in Hasidic costume, but he often has the caricatured features established by anti-Semitism.

We find the figure of the Jew not only in annual ceremonies. One craft which in the past forty years has propagated the stereotype of the Polish Jew abroad as well as in Poland has been folk sculpture and the making of figurines. The Cracovian figurine revived after the war continues its traditional forms, recapitulating the figures of Hasids rocking back and forth as at prayer.[31] The continuation of the established forms of the toy means that its movement, costume and, most important, the lines of the face are perpetuated. Most of the faces invoke anti-Semitic caricatures.

The figures represented by folk sculptors are completely different. Secular folk sculpture, we know, did not flourish in Poland until the post-war years. The subject matter imposed on folk sculptors in the first period was supposed to refer to the pre-1939 period. Naturally, then, the figure of the Jew could not be absent from sculptures representing village life before the war. Because of the commercial success of these figures, they are still frequently made today. Wishing to present figures from the interwar period, folk sculptors often rely on their own memories, recreating a whole range of characters from many different vocations, with their characteristic attributes and in different traditional costumes. Usually they are the

---

[31] These are figurines sold at Salwator Square in Cracow on Easter Monday.

figures with whom Polish society had direct contact: itinerant traders, craftsmen, klezmer musicians and, less often, people representing the interior Jewish world, such as rabbis, yeshiva students, etc. For this reason, in these sculptures we most often meet male figures. Often, especially in the earlier period, the authors of particular sculptures stressed that their works showed particular figures they knew, that they had tried to portray their faces.

Not to multiply the examples from other areas of folk creativity such as writings or proverbs, it is time to consider what kind of stereotype of the Jew is conveyed to us by folk tradition. It certainly is not uniform, but we can point to two basic types: traditional, known in the interwar period and now copied unchanged or very little changed; and new, created at a time when traditional Jewish society has ceased to exist. The latter invokes memories of those times of coexistence, which are also the memories of the youth of the creators of the stereotype and which are subject to all the laws of a remembered time "when we were young and carefree."

Thus, in accord with the basic features of tradition mentioned earlier, this tradition conveys the image of the Jew to us selectively, and we must bear this in mind in reconstructing the life of small-town Jewish communities. However, it seems to me more important to stress that the selection is made not only within the framework of elements of Jewish culture but also within the categories of the time that is being conveyed. According to laws known to psychologists, human memory can purge itself of times that seem alien, cruel and terrifying. For the problem under discussion, the Holocaust is certainly such a time. To perpetuate the memory of that time and to come to terms with what happened to one's Jewish neighbors during the Holocaust would have required a huge emotional investment, and this did not happen in rural or small-town society. The reproduced stereotype is rigid. It shows the Jewish world at a time when it existed. It does not come to terms with the question of what happened to this world, why it is no more. In the material familiar to me, including more than 500 sculptures representing figures of Jews, only a few refer to the time of the Holocaust: "Jewish man and woman part before entering the ghetto," "Jew returning after the war and seeking his family," etc. Thus the Holocaust period is not communicated through the traditional means of repetition of stereotypes, and other means must be found to communicate it.

Monika Adamczyk-Garbowska

General Franco's Daughter

A few years ago, in the first class of a graduate seminar devoted to the problem of how the Holocaust is represented in American films and literature, I conducted a brief survey among the students who had expressed an interest in taking the two-year course. My purpose in making the survey was to find out how much they knew about the Holocaust. These were fourth-year English majors who had completed high school in the mid 1990s, when the history textbooks had already been partially corrected and supplemented, and when the Polish language curriculum included, in addition to Tadeusz Borowski's and Zofia Nałkowska's stories, also Hanna Krall's *To Outwit God* and Andrzej Szczypiorski's *The Beautiful Mrs. Seidenman.*[32] The seminar candidates represented a generation maturing at a time when more and more was being said in the mass media about the Holocaust. This period saw the official observances of the fiftieth anniversary of the Warsaw Ghetto Uprising, the liberation of Auschwitz, and the Kielce pogrom, so I assumed that they should be better grounded than earlier generations attending high school in the 1970s when Jewish

---

[32] Tadeusz Borowski and Zofia Nałkowska both wrote stories with uncompromising depictions of the dehumanizing effects of the Nazi occupation. Borowski survived Auschwitz and Dachau; Nałkowska was a member of Poland's postwar Main Commission for Investigation of German Crimes. *To Outwit God* (Chicago 1992) centers around an interview with Marek Edelman, the last surviving leader of the Warsaw Ghetto Uprising. *The Beautiful Mrs. Seidenman* (New York 1989), set in occupied Poland, portrays the reactions of Polish Christians and of Germans to the plight of the Jews.

subjects were taboo, or in the 1980s when the school textbooks still presented a falsified picture of history despite the emerging fashion for Jewish subjects.

I asked for brief definitions of the Shoah, Umschlagplatz and *Endlösung*, identifications of a few historical figures, organizations and institutions (Anne Frank, Dawid Sierakowiak, Dawid Rubinowicz, Emanuel Ringelblum, Jan Karski, Żegota, Yad Vashem), and the date of the Warsaw Ghetto Uprising.[33] Other questions related to the number of victims of the Auschwitz-Birkenau camps, the origins of the majority of them, and the events of 1968. Finally I asked how many Jews lived in Poland before 1939, and how many do at present.

It turned out that only one of the ten could answer most of the questions (except for the questions about historical figures like Sierakowiak, Rubinowicz and Ringelblum, whom no one was able to identify). Later I found out that the well-informed student also worked as a tour guide and often took groups from Israel through Lublin and Maidanek. Among the rest, only one gave a correct answer about the Shoah (an exhaustive one at that, explaining that it is the Hebrew term for the Holocaust and also saying a few words about Claude Lanzmann's film *Shoah*). Another person, again only one, gave a partial answer about the Umschlagplatz, but most knew what *Endlösung* means. Two gave identifications of Anne Frank, but one of them said she was the daughter of General Franco writing her memoirs. This person, however, was the only student besides the tour

---

[33] Dawid Sierakowiak and Dawid Rubinowicz were ghetto children whose diaries were found after the war. Emanuel Ringelblum, historian of the Warsaw ghetto, wrote reports and collected statistics, memoirs and other documentary material about the situation of the Jews under Nazi occupation, hiding it in buried containers, two of which were recovered after the war. Jan Karski was a Catholic Pole, a resistance hero who entered the Warsaw ghetto and also infiltrated a transit station to Bełżec in order to learn firsthand what was happening to the Jews, later escaping and personally pleading in vain with Allied leaders to stop the Holocaust. Żegota is explained in footnote 12.

guide who could tell who Jan Karski was. They all left a blank space next to the name Żegota, except for one who stated that it was "a district in which Jews were placed." Two gave answers about Yad Vashem, and only one of those was partially correct. For the ghetto uprising only two students gave the correct year of 1943 (without giving the month), one offered a rather lengthy answer about the circumstances of the uprising without giving the date, two gave the year 1941, and the others wrote no answer at all. About the victims of Auschwitz-Birkenau, the answers ranged from 100,000 (the majority Jews) to eight million (the majority Jews or, in another version, members of different nationalities) victims. In fact no one gave correct numbers. On the other hand, almost all of them provided correct answers about March 1968. The last question, about the numbers of Jewish people before the war and now, remained without answer most often; those who tried to provide numbers stated that there are very few Jews in Poland today, perhaps a thousand, and before the war there were perhaps about 30,000, or maybe more than 500,000.[34]

Practically all the seminar participants later wrote excellent master's theses on literary representations of the Holocaust. During the classes and their own research they demonstrated great interest, sensitivity and commitment, and often in hindsight they recalled with laughter or embarrassment how little knowledge about the subject they had brought from school or home.

My observations were confirmed in July 2001 during qualifying interviews for the cultural studies program, a major program that attracts people with broad interests in the humanities, who are often active in various clubs and associations. Despite this, when the interviews touched on Jewish issues – most frequently at the interviewee's initiative, because the examination did not include this particular subject – there were statements

---

[34] Professor Tomaszewski gives the number at almost 3.5 million in his article herein.

like these: they were interested in Jews and the Holocaust because it was a "super subject"; that the term "Holocaust" means "persecution of the Italian minority" (obviously an effect of watching the film *Life Is Beautiful*); that Maidanek is Lublin's "most interesting" or "oldest" monument. Perhaps those last responses should not be so surprising, since I have heard many times from guides I know at the Maidanek Museum that they least like to guide Polish school groups, not so much because of the students as the teachers, as the youth usually have not been prepared for the tour of the camp, and the teachers are cramming the visit to Maidanek between other items on the itinerary, leaving less than an hour for the tour, which should last at least 2.5 hours not including prior preparation. Israeli and German groups are better in comparison, according to the guides, arriving much more prepared.

All these examples show how essential it is to place greater emphasis on teaching about the Holocaust. It is also important for the subject not to be disconnected from the history of the Jews in Poland or Europe. What until recently typified the published guidebooks to various places in Poland, when Jews were presented exclusively in the context of the Holocaust, should have no place in middle school or high school curricula. To convey the tragedy of the Jewish people, an appropriately broad context can be provided by showing the rich culture and history of the Jews and their contribution to Polish and world culture, by pointing out that in prewar Poland there was, besides literature in Polish, a flourishing literature in Yiddish and Hebrew, and by teaching that Poland is the ancestral land not only of ethnic Poles in America and other countries but also of a large part of the Jewish Diaspora scattered around the world.

When I mentioned to an American professor friend, the author of many books about the Holocaust, that the majority of my students had never heard of Anne Frank, he told me, with the ignorance of his own students and the "Americanization" of the Holocaust in mind, "Why give them Anne Frank? After all, you have Dawid Rubinowicz's and Dawid Sierakowiak's diaries in Polish, with much fuller and much more representative descriptions of what happened to the Jews during the Holocaust!"

No doubt he was right about the value of those writings, but those diaries are even less well known in Poland than the diary of Anne Frank. In this country we often hear complaints about foreigners' ignorance of the history of Poland, including the history of the Holocaust. We hear people gripe that Israeli students arrive with a particular ideological stance, that they perceive Poland as a cemetery and not as a country where Jewish culture developed freely for centuries. Undoubtedly there is a great deal of truth in those statements, but before we begin to instruct others it would be worthwhile to start with ourselves and prepare the young generation for an encounter with their own history, often painful, often difficult, but how essential to their intellectual and moral growth.

Hanna Węgrzynek

Every Third One of Us

Walking along Warsaw's streets, I wonder how the city looked before the Second World War. True, I was born many years after it ended, but as a historian I have a need to know the past, and as a Warsovian I try to imagine the bygone city that was called the Paris of the north. They say it was beautiful, more beautiful than today, and different.

Do many Warsaw citizens ask themselves the same question? Probably most are concerned with the here and now. Their roots here, like mine, do not go deep. In most cases their parents or grandparents did not move to Warsaw until after 1945, filling the gap left by those who had departed forever. The family traditions of many modern residents of Warsaw lie elsewhere, and this does not encourage reflection on the look and the character of the city in the past.

In the old photographs we do not see chaotically scattered blocks of grey housing projects. The houses are set tightly side by side, forming the streets. Whole thoroughfares pulsing with life, filled with little shops, eateries and workshops, the likes of which are few today. Most of the surviving photos are of the grandest streets. The life of the side streets is less often documented – and how interesting it must have been!

It has all passed. The people are different as well. They dressed and acted differently then. Women wore hats; it was the fashion, but also a kind of norm imposed by the customs prevailing in certain social groups.

Looking at the pictures, we understand that styles change, but among the crowds of Warsovians from the days of the Second Republic we find yet another difference, one not the result of fashion but of religion and customs. Men in long black topcoats and narrow-brimmed hats. Women in wigs, in dresses completely concealing their elbows and knees. Today we do not meet people dressed like that anymore.

The speech of the prewar streets was also different. It had different sounds, a little harder and grittier, full of the long "w" sound. This was Yiddish, the language of Ashkenazi Jews – Polish Jews. A blend of German, Hebrew and Polish. The smells of the prewar streets were other smells, permeated with goose fat, ginger and garlic. In today's Warsaw there is no way to hear those sounds or sense those smells.

It is hard to believe that there are such places in the world, in Israel or in Brooklyn, New York. There, when the people reminisce about the old Warsaw, the important street names they mention are not Jerozolimskie or Ujazdowskie, but Nalewki, Krochmalna, Gęsia and Żelazna. These streets were the setting of that other world described and popularized by Isaac Bashevis Singer in *Shosha* and *The Family Moskat*. Jewish Warsaw lived beside us Poles for two hundred years. Supposedly the same town, but how remote and unknown.

Before 1939, about 370,000 of the residents, almost a third of Warsaw, were Jews. Can we really appreciate that in every third home Christmas Eve was not celebrated, the Christmas tree was not decorated, and St. Nicholas did not arrive? Completely different holidays were observed, with names that sound foreign to us: Purim, Succoth, Chanukah. Walking down the street, let's imagine that every third person was a member of another culture and religion. Every third person would be someone we could say nothing about today.

The world described by Singer or preserved in a few photographs is one we can no longer find. It perished between October 1940 and May

1943. Tens of thousands of Warsaw citizens, crammed into the ghetto, died of diseases, hunger and repression, and nearly 300,000 were murdered, with systematic and calculated cruelty, in the gas chambers of Treblinka. One third of the residents of the city, the capital of a European state, ceased to exist, along with their language, customs and culture. The way that happened is not a matter of no concern. We cannot fail to know how the life and death of every third one of us Warsovians looked.

The tragic fate of the Warsaw Jews can be contained in an emphatic phrase – the Holocaust, a premeditated atrocity carried out by Nazi Germany. We cannot forget, however, that it was done in our midst. The absence of that memory is our Polish shame. The world of the Warsaw Jews does not exist in the consciousness of the Warsovians who live on Krochmalna, Żelazna and Grzybowska Streets today. It has turned out to be appallingly easy not to know about one third of the residents of the city, who lived here, worked here, and together with Poles created a common history and culture only sixty years ago.

When I attended university, and only then found out that before 1939 as many as 370,000 Jews lived in Warsaw, at first I could not believe it, and later it dawned on me that I had been deceived. In the many books I had read, nothing on the subject was written. I think that this is what has to be changed. I would not want some young resident of Warsaw to someday experience the same feeling that I had when I was already a student in the history department. I would not want them to feel deceived by the "history professionals."

Leszek Hońdo

And the Sun Shone
and Was Not Ashamed

I live in Tarnów, where before the Second World War more than 44 percent of the residents were Jews. Today, little evidence remains to tell us
that Jews helped to build and shape the city, and left a mark on its character. A magnificent Jewish cemetery is preserved. After the war, a monument was erected at a site where mass executions were carried out. Its
main element is a broken column from the New Synagogue, which the
Nazis destroyed. On it is a Hebrew inscription: "The sun shone and was
not ashamed."[35] It is a cry of despair in the face of the tragic events of the
Holocaust of the Jews.

Decades have passed since the Second World War. Today, for children and youth the atrocities of those years, including the Holocaust, are
not so horrifying, neither in the scale of the crime nor in the way it was
carried out. The Holocaust is an extreme example of what racism can lead
to, with its ideology of the superiority of some races, its intolerance of
different groups of people within a single society who differ in their world
views or fundamental political ideas, or its xenophobia, that is, aversion to
or hatred of foreigners. One consequence of World War II was that the
generations growing up after the war had virtually no contact with the

---

[35] The inscription is taken from a poem by Nachman Bialik about the Kishinev
pogrom, and refers to Isaiah 24:23.

problems of ethnic minorities, but it is still important to make them realize the consequences of racism and to place them in the broad context of other ethnic conflicts and the moral norms that apply to the relations and actions of individuals. As we can read in the Universal Declaration of Human Rights, these individuals differ by race, skin color, sex, language, faith, political and other views, nationality, social origin, wealth, birth or other status. These individuals have many different needs which they cannot meet by themselves. They cannot live by themselves in isolation from other people. Contact between them takes two forms: communication and cooperation. In the context of a unifying Europe, these forms take on a new dimension. Every person belongs not only to his family, region or class; his bonds of affiliation to cultural and religious communities extend beyond the boundaries of his country of origin. It is in the perspective of the Holocaust that we see that hatred and hostility toward those who are different or who, on the basis of irrational premises, are outside one's own group, can lead to collective violence and crimes.

Experiences of the Holocaust that relate to the attitudes and behavior of individuals and social groups toward loathsome acts of violence or coldly performed mass executions are important in the moral dimension, for the present and future. The tragic fate of the Jewish people points to the need to seek a new sense of coexistence which overcomes divisions and seeks alternatives to nationalism, racism, extremism and hegemony. Evil springs from ignorance. In the course of school education it is important for a young person to learn not only what differentiates and divides nations, societies and cultures, but what joins them. Showing the richness and values of a multicultural society is one way to inculcate an attitude of respect and tolerance.

The tragic fate of the Jews alludes to the present. Terrible atrocities do not take place in a single moment. They are introduced gradually, with the more or less active or else passive support of the society in which they occur. It begins with a failure to react to derision and humiliation. Later comes denial of rights, and segregation. At the end, the belief emerges that these "others" not only are dispensable but are simply an obstacle to normal life. Thus, teaching about the Holocaust is a reminder that a criminal ideology can arise in any place and at any time. The Holocaust contains the message that it is necessary to react at the beginning, not when it is too late as is the common practice in the modern world.

The example of the Holocaust can be used to show students universal experiences manifested in the attitudes of both individuals and societies: moral choices about good and evil and about the criteria of responsibility for one's actions in the extreme circumstances of war. These decisions were expressed in the different stances taken toward Jews, from self-sacrificing aid often beyond the rational limits of assistance (providing hideouts, food, money and false documents) to vile denunciations and blackmailing of Jews.

Perhaps this kind of sensitizing will put an end to attempts to calculate who owns the world's largest cemetery, Auschwitz-Birkenau – the Jews, more than a million of whom perished there, or the Poles, about 75,000 of whom were murdered there. According to Jean-François Bouthors, such an approach corresponds to the Nazi grasp of the world according to ethnic criteria. Numerical thinking is an affront to each individual victim regardless of ethnic affiliation, for every death was unique. Every murder magnified the contempt for the individual and his differentness.[36]

To explain the horror of genocide is not easy. Many young people come to the conclusion that they will never understand the problem of the Holocaust and therefore do not even try to understand it. Teaching about

---

[36] J.F. Bouthers, "Auschwitz – nakazy i warunki pojednania," in: *Pamięć żydowska, pamięć polska* (papers from a colloquium held in Cracow on June 10–11, 1995), Cracow 1996, p. 155.

the Holocaust should become a permanent element of public education; it should provide reliable knowledge to adults as well as schoolchildren. Its purpose would be to supply arguments that can be used in combatting prejudice and stereotypes, arguments referring to the genocide of which Auschwitz is undeniably a symbol. The student will have to deal with stereotypes in order to handle, for example, the oft-repeated statement (based on the frequent opinion that anti-Semitism was rife in prewar Poland and on ignorance of the nature of the Nazi occupation on Polish soil) that the extermination of Jews would have been impossible if Poles had not collaborated with the Germans in putting Jews to death. The mere fact that the killing of Jews from other European countries took place in Poland was supposed to be proof of this!

Knowledge is needed when bizarre statements are made – in Poland as well – negating the very fact of the genocide, or of particular atrocities in the systematic mass murder of Jews (the "Auschwitz lie"). Followers and imitators of David Irving have surfaced in Poland too. Finally, an argument really very important to me is that we have a responsibility to teach about the Holocaust so long as the word "Jew" remains a term of abuse in the vocabulary of young people.

Sławomir Kapralski

Why Teach About
the Romani Holocaust?

Why is it worthwhile and necessary to teach about the mass murder of
Roma during the Second World War?[37] The immediate answer is that we
are obliged to; we owe it to the Roma and to historical truth. Until recently, the wartime fate of Romani people was a blank page in historiography. Much research is still needed, and previous findings have not been
disseminated broadly enough. Ignorance about what happened to the Roma
has a moral dimension as well: it prevents us from seeing them as victims
of a campaign of racial persecution that was sustained by all the capabili-
ties of modern Europe, and this in turn makes it difficult to free ourselves
from perceiving Roma within the categories of the ingrained stereotypes
that led to their tragedy, stereotypes which still lie at the root of discrimination against them.

In addition to the need to fill gaps in our factual knowledge (and to
reach the broader public with this knowledge), and in addition to the need
for ethical discussion of the moral implications of recognizing the Roma
as victims of Nazi persecution, study of the Romani holocaust also presents an important challenge for social theory. It raises a host of questions

---

[37] I use the term "Roma" in its political and not ethnic sense, as the one recommended by international organizations of Roma to denote all people belonging to groups
who are named Gypsies (*Cyganie*, *Zigeuner*, etc.) by their surrounding communities.
In German-speaking countries, the term *Sinti und Roma* is used in this context.

that can promote reflection on the mechanisms of collective memory, the link between memory and group identity, and the role of contemporary social, political and cultural processes in the formation of new perspectives for understanding the past – and the new meanings that the past acquires in the present.

Thus, in teaching about the Romani holocaust it seems that at least four groups of problems must emerge. The first of these concerns what exactly happened to Roma during World War II. The second is connected with the problem of why Roma did not create a "culture of memory" of their holocaust immediately afterwards, why they themselves stifled the memory of the war or else regarded it as not important. The third group of issues relates to the question of why Roma (or at least certain groups of them) are creating such a culture of memory now, and in what way this process is connected with transformations in Romani culture and in their present-day circumstances. The last group of issues concerns what to call what happened to the Roma during World War II, and what role contemporary discourses attributing meanings to past events plays in interpreting the past: specifically, the dispute about whether the Roma were – on a par with the Jews – Holocaust victims, or whether the persecution they suffered, though tragic, was of a different order than that which befell the Jews and therefore does not fall within the discourse on the Holocaust.

What happened?

In regard to the first group of problems, the forms of Nazi persecution of Roma in the period directly preceding World War II certainly deserve attention. According to certain researchers, one can speak of three such forms: (1) intensification and coordination of already existing means of control and coercion applied to Roma by the authorities; (2) the creation of new guidelines for dealing with Roma, aimed at increasing control and repression, and in consequence at removing Roma from society through an institutionalized policy of deporting them and placing them in concentration camps; and (3) the application of race legislation and policy to Roma, based on an ideology of their biological inferiority which served as the basis for actions leading to their physical annihilation. In part these forms succeed each other, and in part they are simultaneous and overlapping.[38]

Analysis of these problems in the teaching process could lead to a deeper understanding of the phenomenon of Nazi persecution: was it encoded, as it were, in the logic of contemporary society, as Zygmunt Bauman and others maintain, or was it a phenomenon of its own, explainable in terms of the Nazi's anti-Jewish obsession, as for example Yehuda Bauer states. Analyzing the persecution of Roma, and the ideology that justified that persecution, would also reveal the role played by science, as practiced in the Third Reich, in formulating and justifying political decisions, and also in creating a climate of moral acquiescence to the murder of human beings.

Equally important to an understanding of Nazi persecutions is the problem of the process by which decisions about the fate of the Roma were made. The ideological inconsistencies and conflicts between the different institutions that formed the machinery of mass murder are particularly evident in the case of Nazi policy toward Roma. Analyzing this aspect would contribute to a deeper understanding of the tragedy of the Roma and the functioning of the Nazi state.

Another important problem involves examining the extermination process and its different forms. If the fate of Roma in the concentration camps and death camps is fairly well known, much work remains to be done if we are to comprehend the whole extent of the tragedy that befell the Roma, because the majority died in summary executions by the military and police

---

[38] See: G. Lewy, *The Nazi Persecution of the Gypsies*, Oxford–New York 2000, p. 14.

or, especially in the territory of the former Soviet Union, as a result of operations by special units whose task was to exterminate defined categories of people. This leads us to the question of the number of victims. That is extraordinarily difficult if not impossible to establish precisely, because of the lack of exact data on the mass murder and also because estimates of the number of Roma living in Eastern Europe before the war are only approximate. Nevertheless, analysis of the disparities between the numbers given by different researchers (from 200,000 according to Yehuda Bauer, through the most frequently given figure given in current literature, 500,000, to more than a million according to Ian Hancock) would be an instructive example of the objective as well as subjective limits of our knowledge.

Mute memory

The second group of problems opens up a fascinating field of considerations about the relation between history as what happened and history as what has been remembered. Here the focus is the Roma's long silence about their holocaust. That silence existed because traditional Romani culture did not create a discourse in which the Second World War and the tragedy of the Roma could be presented as a singular, unprecedented occurrence, and because historical memory has taken on a very specific form in that culture and has played a lesser role than in other cultures. As an eminent expert on traditional Romani culture, Lech Mróz, writes, memory of the past did not become an element of group identity in that culture; group identity has been based on the effort to maintain the timeless ideal of "the way of a Rom" in the present day, and to defend it against outside influences through a radical separation of the Romani world from the foreign, hostile reality surrounding it.[39] In that reality, history has usually

---

[39] See: L. Mróz, "Niepamięć nie jest zapominaniem. Cyganie-Romowie a holokaust," *Przegląd Socjologiczny*, 2000, vol. XLIX/2, pp. 89–114.

served to legitimize claims to a given territory from which the Roma, through their nomadism or through marginalization and subordination, were excluded. In a sense, Roma had no reason to remember their history as a course of events succeeding each other: their identity was always based on a fairly delicate balance between replicating a certain stable cultural model and adjusting, of necessity, to the situations of daily life and to the changing contexts in which this replication took place. Change came from the outside; it belonged to the foreign, non-Romani world in which Roma endeavored, as much as possible, to live according to their own suprahistorical rules.

The Roma are not "a people without a history"; the point is that an attempt to contain their history in the form of a narrative of historical events which became the shared fate of the group would be something foreign to their traditional culture. Such narratives belong to the non-Romani world. Roma traditionally were separated from that world by a wall of ritual regulations, and were removed from it, often on the other side of walls built of something besides rituals. Thus, to comprehend their fate in the form of *history*, Roma would have had to transgress the boundaries of their world, and that would have amounted to a dramatic threat to the cultural foundations of their existence. For this reason, the memory of the victims of wartime persecution, often vivid and emotionally experienced by individuals and families, could not find cultural expression on the level of discourse of the group as a whole. Thus it was a mute memory, and in that muteness impermanent and fated to disappear gradually.

Moreover, the memory often was expunged from consciousness in a subliminal process of defense of cultural identity; one way of effecting this was to erase the period in which its principles were undermined. Life, survival in harsh conditions, and the continued existence of one's group have been the highest values in traditional Romani culture. Thus, the memory of holocaust times, however vivid and painful in the memories of

individuals and families, was not automatically generalized, institutionalized, and transformed into a buttress of group identity that would unite
(at least potentially) all Roma.

It should also be noted that the Roma are divided into many groups,
often with no communication between them, that until recently their culture depended on oral transmission of tradition, leaving no written sources,
and finally that the majority are people without formal education. All these
factors have contributed to a lack of interest in their own history, that is, in
history as a narrative of events that became the lot of all Roma.

New need for history

In the 1950s this situation began to change. Economic transformations,
a voluntary or coerced shift to a settled style of life, assimilation processes,
the growing role of formal education – all these made traditional Romani
culture, based on replicating in the present the suprahistorical model of
"the way of a Rom," more and more anachronistic, and incompatible with
a reality in which Roma ever more frequently had to come into contact
with the non-Romani society around them on terms set by the latter. In the
absence of options such as effective integration of Roma with the communities in which they lived, the disintegration of traditional Romani culture
meant that intellectuals and Romani activists faced the problem of developing new cultural forms with which Roma could identify in the changed
reality. One such cultural form has been a vision of the Roma as a diaspora
people, having their own history and grounding their modern identity in it.

The vision of history put forward by Romani elites as the domain in
which the modern identity is constructed includes the following elements:
common roots in the culture of India; the common experience of long inter-
action with the European peoples amidst whom the Roma ultimately consti-
tuted themselves as a group (or number of groups); the common experience
of persecution the Roma suffered from others, the culmination and new

dimension of which was the Second World War; and finally, the still-brief but important history of political organizing by Roma.

In presenting such a vision of history, Romani activists wish to stress the antiquity of Romani tradition and culture (the connection with India), while defining themselves as a European people *par excellence* (with an inalienable right to live among the peoples of Europe). They call attention to the modernity of the kind of identity proposed: political self-organization, which takes on many different forms.

The experience of persecution during World War II plays a particular role in this vision. First, making it a fundamental dimension of Romani history is an effort to show the Roma as a people at the center of the most important events in Europe's modern history, not as a marginalized people vegetating outside of history. Second, a historical narrative of the fate of Roma during the war can become an excellent link to unite the different groups into which Roma are divided, by making them aware that in certain historical situations their differences did not matter: they were treated the same (at least in principle) because they were "Gypsies." In this way a uniform narrative of the holocaust period allows the members of different Romani groups, who often do not feel closely associated or are even in conflict, to envision the commonality of fate of the Roma, and this can have important consequences for the forms their political cooperation takes now and in the future. Third, the conception of the history of the Roma as a people which Romani activists have elaborated can contribute to the creation of a paradigm of collective memory in which they can find themselves and can bring together dispersed individual or family memories. In this sense, a history centered around the holocaust of the Roma can create a discourse that will allow forms of expression to be found for the experiences of many Roma who have been silent about their sufferings because they lacked a language to express them until now.

Sufferings in the past are bound up with present-day sufferings. This is the fourth aspect of the vision of history presented here: it can depict contemporary persecutions of Roma as a continuation of the Nazi persecutions and thereby surround them with a similar aura of moral condemnation. Such delegitimation of anti-Romani violence can prove important in education. It allows existing prejudice and acts against Roma to be classed together with the Nazi-inspired racism that is universally condemned. For many students in various European countries whose people suffered during World War II, it will probably be a surprise to learn that they are linked by a commonality of suffering with the generally scorned "Gypsies" (though the Roma suffered to an incomparably greater degree).

Romani activists are fully cognizant of the political weight of such a vision of history. These historical dimensions mentioned above are interwoven with, for example, the political program of the International Romani Union, according to which "The Roma are a legitimate part of European culture and society and ... by virtue of their unique history and problems they deserve special treatment within a European framework. The IRU advocates recognition of the Roma as a nation and is dedicated to building unity around its symbol, a standardized Romani language. The IRU demands the creation of a special status for the Roma and Sinti as a nonterritorial (multistate-based or transnational) minority in Europe, in order to protect a people who experienced a holocaust during World War II and violence, pogroms, and genocide in the present era."[40]

In this manifesto we see the confluence of many earlier-presented elements, comprising a self-definition of modern Roma. The experience of the holocaust appears as one justification of the special status of Roma.

In expanding upon the IRU program, the Romani intellectuals Andrzej Mirga and Nicolae Gheorghe write that "Romani political elites were never

---

[40] A. Mirga, N. Gheorghe, *The Roma in the Twenty-First Century: A Policy Paper*, Princeton: Project on Ethnic Relations 1997, p. 22.

driven to demand their own territory and state. Thus, to legitimize their claim, they advanced other elements of the concept of nation – the common roots of the Romani people, their common historical experiences and perspectives, and the commonality of culture, language and social standing. The experience of the Porraimos – the Romani holocaust during World War II – played an important role in providing the Romani diaspora with its sense of nationhood."[41] Here as well, an extraordinarily important nation-building role is attributed to the experience of the holocaust.

What is its name?

In the context of these quotations, finally it is worth calling attention to the terminology used to describe what happened to the Roma during the Second World War. In the quoted excerpts the term "Romani holocaust" (characteristically, written with a lower-case "h") appears, and also the Romani word "Porraimos," which literally means "the devouring," used by some Romani intellectuals to describe the persecutions suffered by the Roma during the war. Here the terminological problems mirror a very complicated cognitive and ethical problem: what in fact to call what befell the Roma in wartime. In terms of the historical events, we do now have much information about what happened, despite all the limitations on our knowledge. However, the meaning of those events or the definition of the essence of what occurred to the Roma during the war remains a subject of debate.

According to many scholars, both Romani and non-Romani, the Roma were victims of the Holocaust (with a capital "H") as much as the Jews were. These scholars (e.g., Ian Hancock, Gabrielle Tyrnauer, Sybil Milton, Michael Zimmermann) believe that the atrocities committed against the Roma form part of the Nazi plan or intention to completely exterminate "racially inferior" people (Jews and Roma), carried out on a huge scale and

---

[41] Ibidem, p. 18.

employing modern technology and a bureaucracy. For others (Yehuda Bauer, Steven Katz, Elie Wiesel, or recently Guenter Lewy) the Holocaust was the fate of the Jews alone; it was something exceptional, one-of-a-kind, while the persecution of the Roma, undoubtedly cruel though it was, was not aimed at exterminating the entire group on racial grounds. For the latter group of researchers, only certain Roma were condemned to slaughter on racial grounds (so-called "half-breed gypsies"), while the extermination itself was not a planned operation (except for the campaign to sterilize Roma in the Third Reich) but was carried out "incidentally," on the fringes of the extermination of Jews.

It is no wonder that scholars belonging to the first group, especially those who are Romani activists, engage in sharp polemics with such views; this is particularly pronounced in the work of Ian Hancock. He sees the denial of the "right to the Holocaust" to the Roma as a continuation of the centuries-long tradition of the same persecution and marginalization of the Roma that led to their almost complete annihilation during the war. In many official documents of Romani organizations, however, a less conflictive notional convention is applied, according to which the Roma were victims of a holocaust whose relation to the Holocaust of the Jews remains an open question. Another convention involves promulgating the term "Porraimos"; one aim of this is to focus on the Romani experience of their holocaust without reference to what happened to the Jews.

The debate about defining what befell the Roma has, of course, huge practical significance for the process of constructing the modern Romani identity (as well as for the Jewish identity, to the extent that it rests on the memory of the Holocaust as an event that affected only and exclusively the Jews). As a debate essentially about values, it does not seem resolvable on the basis of the social sciences. Analyzing it in the teaching process could, however, direct our attention to the current twists and turns of the memory of the time of slaughter, part of that memory being Holocaust education. In particular, such an analysis would permit an understanding of the dual role of memory: as an instrument for understanding history, and as a justification of the rituals uniting or forming a people. According to Adi Ophir, the author of a work in which that dual role of memory was presented as an antinomy, the more we use the Holocaust as an element of a strategy for constructing or maintaining particular identities, the less chance we have to understand history, to learn the universal aspect of holocaust experiences, and in consequence to have an effective defense against the repetition of tragic events in the future.[42]

In such an understanding, Santayana's famous formula, which everyone visiting the Auschwitz-Birkenau Museum can read, to the effect that those who do not remember the past are condemned to repeat it, would be guilty of Enlightenment naivete. It is not a matter of whether we remember, but of how. Perhaps Nietzsche's vision should therefore be admitted as true: memory enmeshed in the dynamic of our current interests inevitably reproduces the murderous determinism of history. One may ask, though, whether a memory other than memory enmeshed in our interests and in our strategy for constructing identity is at all feasible as a socially important phenomenon. This relates especially to the memory of tragic events that leave traumas in which, as Barbara Misztal writes, "collective identities are most intensively engaged."[43] For the more tragic the past, the less the chance that it will be remembered in a purely intellectual, context-free manner.

For those who teach about the Holocaust, as for their students, it would be worth bearing in mind those conditions of context, and their own role in the process of reproducing memories. Studying the problem of the Romani holocaust can help them in this.

---

[42] A. Ophir, "On Sanctifying the Holocaust. An Anti-Theological Treatise," *Tikkun*, 1988, vol. 2, no. 1, p. 63.

[43] B.A. Misztal, "The Sacralization of Memory," *European Journal of Social Theory* 7 (1), 2004, p. 74.

Andrzej Mirga

For a Worthy Place Among the Victims
The Holocaust and the Extermination of Roma
During World War II

The extermination of Roma during World War II used to be spoken of as
the forgotten Holocaust. Basically it still is. Unlike the Holocaust of the
Jews, or the genocide committed against other peoples and minorities, the
massacre of Roma has not yet entered the canon of modern history curricula. In the majority of European countries it would be useless to search
the school and university history textbooks for even fragmentary information about what happened to this minority in the Nazi era.

Does this in some way implicate the state institutions responsible for
curricula? Does part of the responsibility lie with the historians themselves,
who excluded or overlooked the fate of a "marginal" minority in their studies and thus did not supply the sources and knowledge needed for teaching?
Was it a result of the creation of a dominant narrative of the fortunes of the
nation's citizenry, in which there was no room for the plight of the Romani
minority? Or, finally, does it implicate the Roma themselves, who for one
reason or other did not manage to present the world with their history of
suffering and persecution, so that it would become part of the institutionalized memory of the Second World War in European countries?

History – both the history that researchers write and the living history
formed of memories that are cultivated, maintained and ritualized – is not
something that exists and functions for its own sake. It is often subservi-
ent, it fills a need, or is instrumentalized, particularly when it is ethnic

history. Written and lived history also functions within the broader context of political and international relations, so it is often revalued. Finally, it is a central element of national or group identities, in the maintenance of which institutionalized education plays a fundamental role.

In attempting to answer the questions posed here, it is worth first noting that history is something learned, that historical memory is not only the result of personal experiences and imparted knowledge, but above all its elaboration by historians, and its teaching. States, or ethnic minorities that had the backing of their states, disposed the means to teach history and in this way fashion the historical memory of their national or ethnic communities. The Roma never had such a chance; they did not have their own ethnic school system like other minorities, and in the schools they may have attended, the history of the dominant society was taught, not their own.

In the little Gypsy settlement attached to Czarna Góra village in the Polish part of Spisz, where I was born and spent my childhood, the memory of the war was virtually nonexistent.[44] In my family home, only Mama occasionally returned in memory to that time, and only sporadically. In the evenings, as if casually, she told stories of the Germans and of what had happened to people she knew, or to herself. So we found out that during the war Czarna Góra was in Slovakia (during the time of Fr. Tiso), that our father had been in a P.O.W. camp somewhere in north Germany, liberated by the English.[45] That as a young girl (she was 17 at the outbreak of the war) my mother had survived several roundups in the Gypsy settlement in Czarny Dunajec, that few of the many taken to Auschwitz had returned; one of the victims did return, and had a camp number tattooed on her forearm... For us children, those fragments of Mama's wartime recollections left impressions of what our parents had experienced. School

---

[44] Spisz: a region in the Western Carpathians.

[45] Jozef Tiso: President of the collaborationist government of Slovakia from 1939 to 1945; executed for treason and war crimes.

and history lessons filled out the picture of the horrors of World War II, but did not lead to an understanding of what nazism and the war were for the Roma, and why the Roma were murdered and persecuted... The individual memory of the victims, even if present in the form described above, was not generalized in the form of reflection on the fate of the Roma during the war. For that would have required going outside the individual framework of memory to trace and reconstruct the course and scale of events, to discover existing sources and compile reference works; thus it would have required an elite able to put together the experiences and generalize them, an elite able to create and disseminate a historical narrative.

Historiography and the teaching of history cannot proceed without the educated elites that perform those tasks. The Roma had no such elites, neither before nor directly after the war. Nor were there individuals among the Roma who would have recorded their personal tragedy or the group's tragedy in memoirs, or left traces or documents of those experiences in some other form. The cases of Papusza and the poem "Bloody Tears" or of Karl Stojka's Auschwitz pictures are exceptions.[46] This absence of elites, especially the absence of Romani historians, is still felt today. The majority of works devoted to the extermination of Roma are by non-Romani historians.

Shaping historical awareness is also the task of political elites. A few Romani ethnic organizations began to emerge in the 1960s and 1970s in

---

[46] Papusza (Bronisława Wajs), 1908?–1987: Romani singer, poet and composer of songs, some of whose work was translated to Polish and published by Jerzy Ficowski, including the autobiographical ballad "Bloody Tears: What We Went Through Under the Germans in Volhynia in the Years '43 and '44"; Papusza, *Lesie, ojcze mój*, Warsaw 1990, pp. 66–81. Ficowski was the first to write about the extermination of Roma, in: *Cyganie Polscy*, Warsaw 1953. See also an article about Papusza by Gigi Thobodeau at www.kmareka.com/growinganewskin.htm

Karl Stojka (1931–2003): Rom from eastern Austria, imprisoned in Auschwitz-Birkenau at the age of 12, who made paintings in his later years depicting the wartime sufferings of his family and people; *The Story of Karl Stojka: A Childhood in Birkenau*, Washington, D.C. 1992.

the countries of Europe. The first congress of Roma, held in London in 1971, initiated a wider Romani ethnic movement. This led to the establishment of the International Romani Union (IRU) in 1972. The Romani elites associated in the IRU raised the question of the extermination of Roma and began to demand a worthy place among the victims of nazism. IRU efforts for recognition of the Holocaust of Roma became part of the construction of broader historical awareness in Romani society.

The lack of Romani intellectual or political elites after the war does not furnish a strong argument to explain the historians' silence or indifference about the fate of this minority in the course of the war. More significant, it would appear, was the way the Nuremberg trials dealt with the mass murder of Roma, on the one hand, and on the other hand the outcome of efforts by German Sinti and Roma to obtain compensation for war victims from the newly established Federal Republic of Germany in the 1950s and 1960s.

In the Nuremberg trials, the sequence of events and the scale of the mass murder of Roma were treated only marginally; there was not a single Rom among the witnesses, and the documents and other testimony confirming the extermination of Roma were few. In the indictment against Hermann Goering, based on Article 6 of the Charter of the International Military Tribunal (IMT) (conspiracy, crimes against peace, war crimes and crimes against humanity), the Roma were mentioned in the war crimes charge, but did not appear in the charge for crimes against humanity. In Judge Robert H. Jackson's opening statement, the Roma were mentioned in the context of the experiments in the concentration camps (the first victims were four Romani women in Dachau). In the closing statements of the English, French and Russian prosecutors, there were references to "genocide" committed against Roma, but the Roma were not mentioned, as for example the Jews were, in the wording of Goering's sentence.[47]

---

[47] M. Rooker, *The International Supervision of Protection of Romany People in Europe*, Nijmegen 2002, pp. 38–51.

More attention and space was devoted to the Roma in successive trials: the so-called medical trials, those against the justice system, and against the Einsatzgruppen. The ones on trial were Nazis of lower rank, however. Thus the Nuremberg trials did not become a watershed for the Roma as they did for the Jews; the Holocaust of the Jews was proven and was judged, while the extermination of Roma was merely noted. Not until the trial of Adolf Eichmann in 1962 in Jerusalem were the crimes against the Roma broadly presented and proven. That was still not enough of a stimulus for historians to turn their interest to the Roma and undertake laborious research into the plight of this community during the war.

The efforts by German Sinti and Roma in the Federal Republic of Germany to get reparations and compensation for the persecution and repression, fruitless for decades, illustrate the difficulties facing this minority – and any historians who may take up the subject. The new Germany was obliged by the Allies to compensate the victims of nazism. This obligation was fulfilled under three federal laws. The first was enacted in 1953, and the following two were revisions of the first, in 1956 and 1963.[48] They dealt with reparations for victims of persecution for political, racial, religious and ideological reasons. If the question of reparations to Jews for the Holocaust was clear, and settled through direct negotiations with the Claims Conference (Conference on Jewish Material Claims Against Germany), the comparable demands of German Sinti and Roma were challenged by the authorities of the new Germany. They could only direct individual lawsuits to the German courts, invoking the laws mentioned above. The German courts dismissed these claims on principle, stating that they had not been persecuted on racial but rather on social grounds, as "asocial." In other words, the German courts questioned the fact of the genocide perpetrated against this minority – the preplanned policy of ex-

---

[48] United States Holocaust Memorial Museum, German Compensation for National Socialist Crimes, at: www.ushmm.org/assets/frg.htm

termination for racial reasons.[49] This view was widely shared by German society, its elites included. Having no strong support in the Nuremberg trial judgements, disposing no broad base of sources documenting the crimes committed by the Nazis against this minority, having no support from influential historians and German political circles, up to the early 1980s the Sinti and Roma were unable to seriously challenge that interpretation applied by the German courts.

A few voices of support came from Jewish victims of persecution who had witnessed the extermination of Roma. Simon Wiesenthal is one example. In the early 1960s he began to collect documents attesting to the Holocaust of Roma. In 1965 he transferred them to the Central Office for the Investigation of Nazi Crimes in Ludwigsburg. In his book from 1967, *The Murderers Among Us*, he included a chapter on the persecution of Roma.[50] Similar motivations – support for the efforts of German Sinti and Roma before the German courts – spurred Donald Kenrick and Gratton Puxon to gather together all the available archival sources and articles on the subject from many countries of Europe. The result of their research was the book *The Destiny of Europe's Gypsies*, published in 1972.[51] It helped break through the dominant narrative of the Holocaust in the decades that followed. It also supplied strong arguments to the Roma themselves, in their work to get Germany to recognize the persecutions of that community as crimes of genocide. In this process a special role was played by the Heidelberg organization Verband Deutscher Sinti und Roma, and its leader Romani Rose. With support from the German organization

---

[49] S. Milton, "Persecuting the Survivors: The Continuity of Antigypsism," in: S. Tebbut (ed.), *Sinti and Roma: Gypsies in German Speaking Society and Literature*, Oxford 1998.

[50] J. Wechsberg (ed.), *The Murderers Among Us. The Simon Wiesenthal Memoirs*, New York 1967.

[51] D. Kenrick, G. Puxon, *The Destiny of Europe's Gypsies*, New York 1972.

Gesellschaft für bedrohte Völker (Society for Endangered Peoples) of Göttingen, German Sinti and Roma organized a number of spectacular actions intended to shake up German public opinion. It was this kind of activity, like the demonstration at the former Bergen-Belsen concentration camp in 1979 and the hunger strike at Dachau in 1980, or the 3rd Roma World Congress in Göttingen in 1982, that led Helmut Schmidt's government in that year to make a declaration acknowledging Germany's responsibility for the Holocaust of Sinti and Roma, affirming that they had been persecuted on racial grounds.[52] One consequence of Schmidt's declaration was the establishment of government-supported foundations in the German states, whose task was to review claims and pay compensation to German Sinti and Romani citizens who had been victimized by Nazi persecutions.

Schmidt's declaration broke down a certain mental barrier, at least among the political elites in Germany, not to say the whole of society. Jewish circles frequently resisted acknowledging that the mass murder of Roma was perpetrated out of the same racial motivations as in their own case. According to Simon Wiesenthal, when the anniversary of the liberation of the Bergen-Belsen camp was observed in 1985, the Central Council of Jews in Germany refused the request of German Sinti for a place among the speakers. Wiesenthal's personal intervention proved fruitless, so he turned to then-Chancellor Helmut Kohl, who referred to the tragedy of the Sinti and Roma in his address.[53] Similarly, when the Council of the United States Holocaust Memorial Museum in Washington was estab-

---

[52] Y. Matras, "The Development of the Romani Civil Rights Movement in Germany, 1945–1996," in: S. Tebbut (ed.), *Sinti and Roma: Gypsies in German Speaking Society and Literature*, Oxford 1998.

[53] S. Wiesenthal, "Jews and Gypsies: Genocide of Non-Jewish Victims in the Holocaust as Seen by a Survivor of the Holocaust," in: I.W. Charny (ed.), *Encyclopedia of Genocide*, vol. I, Santa Barbara, California 1999, pp. 502–505.

lished in 1979, there was no Romani representative among its members. Years later, in 1987, William Duna was invited to the Council, and he was followed by Ian Hancock in 1997. The barrier has been breached among the historians as well; more and more researchers in Germany and other countries are tackling topics related to the Romani Holocaust. With his many publications on the subject, Ian Hancock has played a special role in this process.

The gains of German Sinti and Roma became the gains of Roma in other European countries a decade later, after the collapse of communism and the Berlin Wall. Today, in anniversary observances commemorating the Holocaust of the Roma or Jews, representatives of both communities participate. The annual ceremony on August 2nd at Auschwitz-Birkenau – the date of the liquidation of the so-called *Zigeunerlager* ("Gypsy camp") – is already a permanent element of the observance schedule there. Every year it gathers multitudes of Roma from all over Europe, as well as representatives of the national executives and governments of many countries, including Israel. In 1997, the Documentation and Cultural Centre of German Sinti and Roma was established in Heidelberg;[54] there is a permanent exhibition at the Auschwitz-Birkenau State Museum; and the United States Holocaust Memorial Museum in Washington now devotes more attention to the Holocaust of Roma. In this way, gradually the memory of the Romani tragedy is becoming part of the institutionalized memory of the Holocaust. It is high time for it likewise to become part of the historical memory of both Roma and non-Roma. Incorporating the history of Roma, including the history of their persecution and their Holocaust, in core curricula, can bring this about, for "it is understanding, not the refusal of understanding, that makes it possible to prevent a repetition of the horror."[55]

---

[54] See: www.sintiundroma.de/english/html
[55] T. Todorov, *Facing the Extreme: Moral Life in the Concentration Camps*, New York 1996, p. 277.

Natalia Aleksiun

The History and Memory of the Holocaust
The Central Jewish Historical Commission

Icchak Schipper, a historian of Polish Jewry, ended up in the Maidanek concentration camp. Explaining a point to his fellow prisoner Aleksander Donat, he said this:

> ...everything depends on who transmits our testament to future generations, on who writes the history of this period. History is usually written by the victor. What we know about murdered peoples is only what their murderers vaingloriously cared to say about them. Should our murderers be victorious, should they write the history of this war, our destruction will be presented as one of the most beautiful pages of world history, and future generations will pay tribute to them as dauntless crusaders. Their every word will be taken for gospel. Or they may wipe out our memory, as if we had never existed, as if there had never been a Polish Jewry, a Ghetto in Warsaw, a Maidanek.[56]

Of the Holocaust testimonies I know, Schipper's words are particularly moving, even though he does not directly describe the atrocities committed at that time. Schipper realized that preserving documentation, allowing the fate and the murder of particular families and communities of Polish Jews to be reconstructed, would shape the way they would be remembered.

---

[56] A. Donat, *The Holocaust Kingdom. A Memoir,* New York, Chicago, San Francisco 1965, p. 210.

During the occupation, in fact, many Jews were already making efforts to leave some trace after the abominations that were being perpetrated; they kept diaries and left written testimony. According to Emanuel Ringelblum, "during this terrible war, everyone generally has been keeping diaries."[57] In many ghettos, labor camps and even the death camps, Jews strove to record and store official documents as well as their personal statements. Efforts were undertaken individually, and archives were organized. The largest archive, *Oneg Shabbat*, was established in Warsaw as early as the autumn of 1939, by the historian and social activist Emanuel Ringelblum.

After the years of persecution and the daily struggle to survive, the Polish Jews who remained alive placed great importance on collecting historical documentation of the Holocaust. They saw in it not only a form of vengeance against those guilty of the crimes committed against the Jews, but also as a moral duty to those who had perished. With this motivation, Filip Friedman began to gather materials on the history and the slaughter of the Jews in Lwów in the summer of 1944, shortly after the city was liberated from German occupation. One of the first institutions organized by a group of surviving Jews in Vilnius was a Jewish museum, where Abba Kovner and Abram Sutzkever collected Holocaust-related documents.

Among the efforts undertaken by Polish Jews who survived the Holocaust, the work of the Central Jewish Historical Commission occupies a special place. In Lublin on August 29, 1944, only a month after the town's liberation from German occupation, five Polish Jews met to discuss the creation of a *historishe komisye* under the Jewish Committee

---

[57] Emanuel Ringelblum recalls the general phenomenon of writing memoirs in the Warsaw ghetto in: E. Ringelblum, *Kronika getta warszawskiego: wrzesień 1939 – styczeń 1943*, Warsaw 1983, p. 490.

operating in the city. Four months later the Historical Commission was renamed the Central Jewish Historical Commission in Poland, with Dr. Filip Friedman at the head. In March 1945 the Commission's head-quarters was moved from Lublin to Łódź. In the spring and summer of 1945, regional, provincial and local historical commissions were established in Cracow, Warsaw, Białystok, Katowice, Gliwice, Bytom, Będzin and Przemyśl. Correspondents were dispatched to many other localities, including Częstochowa, Wrocław, Piotrolesie and Parczew. At the peak of its activity the Commission had 25 branches.

The Commission's statute called for the establishment of an archive and library, and publication of materials describing what befell Jews during the Second World War, for the purpose of assembling the information needed to pursue war criminals. One of the most important areas of the Commission's activity was the creation of the archive. Among the materials it amassed were photographs, documents, accounts by victims and witnesses of Nazi crimes, poetry, memoirs, descriptions of children's games, and sayings. Songs sung in the ghettos, camps and partisan units could be found in the archive. Also collected were ghetto seals and coins, ritual objects, and even urns with the ashes of murdered Jews, destined for the future museum. By 1946 the Commission archive already held about 7,000 documents and more than 3,000 photographs.

One important task the founders and staff of the Commission set for themselves was to record survivor accounts. At its founding meeting in the autumn of 1944, the participants decided to collect testimonies of Jews who survived the German occupation, and they prepared a questionnaire covering their experiences. In a report of the Central Jewish Historical Commission's activities from 1946, Noe Grüss noted that 1,800 testimonies had been taken in Commission offices, private homes and orphanages. The Society of Friends of the Central Historical Commission made an appeal to "all Jews in Poland":

We, the small handful of Jews saved by a miracle from the hands of the murderers, are duty-bound to do everything in our power so that those horrors experienced, that appalling time, will be preserved forever for future generations.... It is the duty of every Jew to describe his experience, because every living, conscious Jew experienced the various events differently. Whoever cannot write should immediately go to the nearest Historical Commission, where his experiences will be recorded. No instance of cruelty, no instance of self-sacrifice should be left untold.[58]

One of the Commission's main goals was to research the history of the Polish Jews under German occupation and to educate both Jews and the broader Polish public on the subject.[59] A library was established, and the Commission began to publish primary sources as well as the first historical works. The Commission initiated research about the perpetrators, witnesses and Jewish victims. One of its aims was to disseminate research on the crimes committed against Jews during the war. The Commission published many books and articles that set the direction of Holocaust research. Among the first were compilations of primary source material, including the memoirs of Róża Bauminger, Gusta Dawidsohn-Draenger, and Noemi Szac-Wajnkranc.

Holocaust education entails many challenges. One is to avoid the danger of focusing all attention on detailed study of the atrocities, probing the mechanisms that made Nazi ideology assume one form rather than another. Teaching about the Holocaust can also be an opportunity to remember its victims. In one of his lectures, Elie Wiesel spoke of the loneliness of those dying: "to be remembered, that was all they wanted."[60]

---

[58] Archiwum Żydowskiego Instytutu Historycznego, CKŻP, Komisja Historyczna, 336/ 31, Sprawozdania Towarzystwa Przyjaciół Żydowskiej Komisji Historycznej, pp. 21–22.

[59] N. Grüss, *Rok pracy Centralnej Żydowskiej Komisji Historycznej*, Łódź, 1946, p. 9.

[60] E. Wiesel, "The Holocaust as literary inspiration," in: *Dimensions of the Holocaust. Lectures at Northwestern University*, Evanston, 1996, p. 16.

Both during the Holocaust and after the war's conclusion, Polish Jews did much to rescue the memory of those people. I think that these very efforts to pass on the truth about the crimes committed, to safeguard the memory of Jewish life under German occupation, impose a moral obligation to convey that truth, and to remember. In this sense, the attempts to communicate the truth about the fate of the Jews under German occupation constitute a fascinating page in the history of Jewish resistance.

Jolanta Ambrosewicz-Jacobs

Attitudes of Polish Youth Toward the Holocaust
Research from 1997–2000

The Holocaust is part of Polish history, but not enough about it is taught in the schools. When it is taught, usually the subject is not related to current events or to concern for the shape of the future.

Data from research done in 1997, 1998 and 2000 permit an examination of the attitudes of young Poles toward the Holocaust, attitudes which reflect knowledge about and emotions elicited by the Holocaust.[61]

The subjects in the 1997 research were 568 primary and secondary school students from southern Poland. The subjects in 1998 and 2000 were a random, representative national sample totaling 1,002 students. The research employed a questionnaire with 78 items including 14 open questions, plus nine questions to establish the student's sex, age, place of residence, type of school, average grades, parents' education, religion, degree of religiosity, and frequency of church attendance.

---

[61] Earlier national research, on adult Poles' attitudes toward Jews and the Holocaust, was done in 1992; see: I. Krzemiński (ed.), *Czy Polacy są antysemitami? Wyniki badania sondażowego*, Warsaw 1996. The 1997 research was financed by a grant from the Rabbi Marc Tanenbaum Foundation for the Advancement of Interreligious Understanding. The data from 1998 and 2000 were collected and processed in the "Alternative methods of education in overcoming ethnic prejudices" project (grants from the Jagiellonian University Central Research Fund from 1998, 1999 and 2000, and from the Open Society Foundation – RSS 122/98).

The questionnaire was administered to groups and filled in voluntarily and anonymously in 93 randomly selected secondary schools in ten regions of Poland.[62] The questionnaire took 45 minutes to complete. The same questionnaire was given in three experimental and three control classes at high schools in Cracow, Warsaw and Łomża.

In 1997 the statement that knowledge of the crimes committed in Auschwitz should be conveyed to the next generations as a lesson for mankind was affirmed by 90.3% of the total sample, 94.9% of the secondary school students, and 100% of the students from classes with innovative experimental programs formed at the initiative of individual teachers. In 1998, 88% of the national sample of 1,002 students affirmed a similar statement. More students (95.8%) from the experimental classes, which had course content going beyond the standard curriculum and designed to increase openness to ethnic and religious minorities, affirmed the state-

Table 1.
"Knowledge of the crimes committed in Auschwitz and other concentration camps should be conveyed to the next generations as a lesson for all mankind." Responses in experimental classes from 1998 and 2000.

Year of survey	Group	Number of answers	Yes (%)	No (%)
1998	All*	71	95.8	4.2
	Warsaw	17	94.1	5.9
	Cracow	30	93.3	6.7
	Łomża	24	100.0	—
2000	All*	69	98.6	1.4
	Warsaw	17	100.0	—
	Cracow	28	100.0	—
	Łomża	24	95.8	4.2

* Only students who participated in both years are included in these statistics.

---

[62] The questionnaires were administered by the CEM Institute for Market and Public Opinion Research of Cracow. Only two schools declined to participate in the survey.

ment in 1998; two years later in 2000, all the students from the experimental classes in Warsaw and Cracow affirmed the statement (Table 1).

Nevertheless, 57.1% of the total 1997 sample (65.9% of small-town elementary school students and 64.1% of academic high school students) were not bothered by or ashamed of anti-Jewish graffiti, and 16.8% found it amusing. A year later, 30.6% of the larger, national sample disagreed with the statement that anti-Jewish graffiti was disturbing or shameful to them, but only 6.1% of the experimental class students and none of the Warsaw experimental class students responded that way. The difference between the 1997 and 1998 results might be attributable to the methodol-

Table 2.
"Many of the crimes in Auschwitz and other concentration camps did not really take place." Responses in 1998 and 2000.

NATIONAL SAMPLE AND EXPERIMENTAL CLASSES IN 1998

Group		Number of answers	Yes (%)	No (%)
National sample	All	962	12.8	87.2
	Academic	314	7.6	92.4
	Technical	375	11.5	88.5
	Vocational	273	20.5	79.5
Experimental classes		78	2.6	97.4

EXPERIMENTAL CLASSES

Year	Group	Number of answers	Yes (%)	No (%)
1998	All*	68	2.9	97.1
	Warsaw	16	—	100.0
	Cracow	29	—	100.0
	Łomża	23	8.7	91.3
2000	All*	71	1.4	98.6
	Warsaw	17	—	100.0
	Cracow	30	—	100.0
	Łomża	24	4.2	95.8

* Only students who participated in both years are included in these statistics.

ogy (the 1998 survey had five possible answers to the question, and the 1997 survey only three), but the answers in the experimental classes seem to evince those students' greater awareness.

The breakdown of responses from the 1998 survey reveals that 12.8% of the total sample (7.6% of academic high school students, 20.5% of vocational students, and only two students from experimental classes) believed that many of the crimes of Auschwitz and other concentration camps did not really take place. None of the experimental class students in Cracow and Warsaw expressed any doubt in either 1998 or 2000 that the genocidal crimes took place (Table 2).

For comparison – and we should not take comfort from this – 28.8% of 223 students from three Manhattan schools surveyed in 1997 gave answers expressing doubt about the Holocaust.[63] In Sweden, 8,000 students from 120 schools were surveyed, and 34% of them were not certain that the Holocaust had really occurred.[64] The Swedish government's reaction to this was swift, however: an informative book about the Holocaust was sent to every home.

In the 1998 national survey, one question was "Do you think the Poles helped the Jews during the war?" The most frequent answers checked were "yes, as much as they could" (46.2%) and "hard to say" (42.9%). Only 9.3% (28.8% in the experimental classes) stated "they could have done more," and 1.6% said "they didn't help at all" (Table 3).

Opinions about whether Poles could have rescued more Jews during the war were polarized. More than half of the surveyed youth were unsure or avoided answering. To understand what went on during the war, students definitely should learn more about Polish-Jewish relations in the past.

---

[63] Data from my survey evaluating the educational program of the Simon Wiesenthal Center in New York. See more in: J. Ambrosewicz-Jacobs, C. Yung, "What Is in the Way? Teaching About the Holocaust in Post-1989 Poland," in: *Remembering for the Future: The Holocaust in an Age of Genocides*, Basingstoke 2001.

[64] *Gazeta Wyborcza*, June 13, 1997, p. 5.

Table 3.

"Do you think the Poles helped the Jews during the war?"

Responses in 1998 and 2000.

NATIONAL SAMPLE AND EXPERIMENTAL CLASSES IN 1998

Group		Number of answers	Yes, as much as they could (%)	Hard to say (%)	They could have done more (%)	They didn't help at all (%)
National sample	All	962	46.2	42.9	9.3	1.6
	Academic	310	50.3	36.5	11.6	1.6
	Technical	377	49.6	39.5	10.1	0.8
	Vocational	275	36.7	54.9	5.5	2.9
Experimental classes		73	57.5	13.7	28.8	—

EXPERIMENTAL CLASSES

Year	Group	Number of answers	Yes, as much as they could (%)	Hard to say (%)	They could have done more (%)	They didn't help at all (%)
1998	All*	64	56.2	17.2	26.6	—
	Warsaw	14	50.0	14.3	35.7	—
	Cracow	28	67.9	3.6	28.5	—
	Łomża	22	45.5	36.4	18.1	—
2000	All*	64	70.3	6.2	23.5	—
	Warsaw	14	42.9	14.3	42.8	—
	Cracow	29	86.2	3.4	10.4	—
	Łomża	21	66.7	4.8	28.5	—

* Only students who participated in both years are included in these statistics.

The attitudes of Polish students toward the Holocaust, toward Jews, and toward foreigners and ethnic minorities are interrelated. The lack of consistency in their answers concerning the Holocaust can be attributed to their lack of knowledge, and to emotions bound up with patriotism and their attachment to an image of the special role of the Poles in history. Another factor in the inconsistency of attitudes could be socially inherited conflicts elicited by the subject of the Holocaust, and the defense mecha-

Table 4.

"Do the Jews deserve special treatment and care because of the losses and suffering they sustained during the war?"
Responses in 1998 and 2000.

NATIONAL SAMPLE AND EXPERIMENTAL CLASSES IN 1998

Group		Number of answers	Yes (%)	Don't know (%)	No (%)
National sample	All	993	7.4	41.4	51.2
	Academic	327	4.6	33.9	61.5
	Technical	389	9.0	43.4	47.6
	Vocational	277	8.3	47.3	44.4
Experimental classes		81	8.6	28.4	63.0

EXPERIMENTAL CLASSES

Year	Group	Number of answers	Yes (%)	Don't know (%)	No (%)
1998	All*	71	7.0	29.6	63.4
	Warsaw	17	5.9	29.4	64.7
	Cracow	30	13.3	26.7	60.0
	Łomża	24	—	33.3	66.7
2000	All*	69	14.5	26.1	59.4
	Warsaw	16	25.0	37.5	37.5
	Cracow	29	10.3	20.7	69.0
	Łomża	24	12.5	25.0	62.5

* Only students who participated in both years are included in these statistics.

nisms used to attenuate those conflicts. The survey data could also be interpreted as an expression of a peculiar type of contest for moral superiority between Poles and Jews, which would support a thesis put forward by a Warsaw research group under the direction of Ireneusz Krzemiński,[65] regarding the fear that acknowledging another nation's greater losses and

---

[65] I. Krzemiński (ed.), *Czy Polacy są antysemitami...*, pp. 20, 103–114, 193.

suffering might diminish one's own losses and suffering. Of the total national sample, 51.2% negatively answered the question about whether Jews should merit special treatment and care because of their wartime losses and suffering (Table 4).

When the Nazis created the ghettos and death camps, they located the majority of them on occupied Polish territory. The Holocaust is part of Polish history, but current curricula still do not direct the attention of young Poles to the facts of the Holocaust and its implications for the future.

In explaining the inconsistency of answers related to the Holocaust, we should take developmental factors into account (the subjects were 16 to 18 years old, a period when changes in self-image and social perspectives occur), and should also consider the teenagers' opinions about the reasons for the anti-Semitic attitudes of some people. Among the reasons the students gave are these:

- negative opinions of Jews in the community (64.4%)
- conflicts from the past (51.6%)
- some people's aversion to foreigners (50.2%)
- lack of direct contact with Jews (46.9%).[66]

A typical scapegoating cliche ("the Jews' own responsibility for that attitude") was not the most frequently selected reason (14.4%). It seems that the students repeat opinions they hear at home or in the media. These opinions are not necessarily deep-rooted – another explanation of inconsistent answers.[67]

Like most teaching in Poland, teaching about the Holocaust is not linked to the students' natural curiosity. History instruction that relies on imagination and interest is more effective than transmitting information

---

[66] The respondents had nine answers to choose from, and they could pick more than one or write their own opinion.

[67] Such an opinion was expressed by the American psychologist Lane Arye, who lived in Warsaw for four years in the 1990s.

about historical events from textbooks. Facts are important, but large numbers do not say everything. It has to be remembered that each victim of the genocide died individually and only once. That is why documents from witnesses, such as memoirs, diaries, photographs, drawings and films, should be used to a much greater extent in history classes. Unfortunately, oral history does not enter the curriculum until post-secondary school, and not in every university.

The Holocaust can be a topic of integrated teaching in the form of multidisciplinary projects. It should not be limited to a subject heading in a textbook or a collection of historical facts. Teaching about the Holocaust requires exploration of the context, the use of primary sources, and analysis of people's moral choices and attitudes toward the Holocaust and postwar reactions to it.[68] This teaching can go on not only in history or literature classes but also in civics or religion courses.

In teaching about the Holocaust it is essential to make reference to current manifestations of anti-Semitism, combined with analysis of the sources of prejudice and hatred, which in conducive circumstances can lead to discriminatory behavior. Anti-Semitism should have disappeared after the Holocaust, but it did not, and that is one reason we should teach about the Holocaust.

---

[68] M. Weitzman, "Coming to Grips with Teaching the Holocaust," *Momentum: Journal of the National Catholic Educational Association*, 1988, no. 2, pp. 55–57.

Holocaust-Related Topics on the Internet

The Internet offers new opportunities for Holocaust teaching and learning. The sources on the subject are very extensive, particularly in English and German, ranging from historical treatments to primary sources and pictorial material. Internet discussion groups provide a worldwide forum for the exchange of views and information.

The small selection of web sites listed below is an expanded version of a list of descriptions compiled by students Anna Dziadyk (sociology) and Andrzej Cała (psychology) for a course entitled "Anatomy and dynamics of prejudice" given by Jolanta Ambrosewicz-Jacobs during the 2000/2001 academic year in the Institute of Polish Philology of the Jagiellonian University. Some of the sites and their institutions are devoted exclusively to the Holocaust, some include it as part of a larger program, and others have related interests such as anti-Semitism, teaching tolerance, or the Jewish community in Poland today. More links can be found at http://tolerance.research.uj.edu.pl

Amcha. National Israeli Center for Psychosocial Support of Survivors of the Holocaust and the Second Generation

http://www.amcha.org

Languages: English, Hebrew

"Amcha" is a codeword Jews used to identify each other as survivors after the Holocaust. The organization that goes by that name in Israel is a support network of psychologists, educators and social workers, for survivors and their families. It is focused on the psychological effects of experiences connected with the Shoah.

The site contains links to a selection of articles on post-traumatic stress disorder and survivors (particularly in regard to children), and the next generation living with the legacy of the Shoah. Some of the material can be downloaded as Word documents or purchased.

The site also offers a detailed calendar of conferences. There is a section to help with searches for relatives, and providing information on recovery of property or art lost during the war.

American Friends of the Ghetto Fighter's House

http://www.friendsofgfh.org

Language: English

This organization supports the Ghetto Fighters House Museum in Israel, publicizes the history of Jewish resistance during the war, and educates. It promotes the International Book-Sharing Project for joint study of Holocaust literature between schools in Israel and the United States. It gives lectures and seminars for teachers. The site offers books for sale, the majority devoted to Holocaust resistance and to Janusz Korczak.[69]

---

[69] Janusz Korczak (Henryk Goldschmidt) was a Polish Jew, army officer, physician, educator and writer, who pioneered an education methodology based on respect for children. Refusing a chance to save his own life when the orphanage he ran in the Warsaw ghetto was liquidated, he went with the children under his care to death in Treblinka.

Anne Frank House

http://www.annefrank.nl

Languages: Dutch, English, German, Spanish

The Anne Frank Museum was created in the home where she hid and wrote her diary during the war. Its educational effort is directed mainly to young people. The site includes fragments of the diary, a biography of Anne, and several articles (one is about the role of a sense of humor in counteracting prejudice).

Anti-Defamation League

http://www.adl.org

Language: English

The Anti-Defamation League, ADL, aims to fight anti-Semitism, bigotry and extremism. It prepares educational programs and resources to help combat prejudice and build tolerance toward others. The organization, created in 1913, sets out to fight intolerance and to disseminate knowledge about the Holocaust, human rights and religious freedom, as well as to inform about terrorist threats, hate on the Internet, and the harmful effects of hate symbols. The World of Difference Institute, functioning on the web site, prepares primary and secondary teachers to fight prejudice. The Campus of Difference plays that role in higher education, and the Workplace of Difference in private and state institutions. The ADL site offers exercises, guides and programs aimed at helping develop tolerance and mutual understanding. The organization has an on-line store, where it is possible to order magazines, books, videos and educational resources for teaching about the Holocaust, multiculturalism and human rights.

Anti-Semitism and Xenophobia Today

http://www.axt.org.uk

Language: English

The Anti-Semitism and Xenophobia Today (AXT) Internet site publishes analyses regarding the presence of racism, xenophobia and especially anti-Semitism, considered against the backdrop of the more general social and political contexts in which such manifestations occur. AXT is an integral part of the Institute for Jewish Policy Research (JPR) – a group of independent experts and intellectuals based in London. JPR has both a research and an opinion-forming role, influencing the political scene. The JPR staff use the AXT site to disseminate analyses. The site's content includes reports and educational material on demographics, migration trends, media and culture, court verdicts and significant manifestations of discrimination.

The Association of Roma in Poland

http://www.stowarzyszenieromow.hg.pl

Language: Polish

The Association of Roma in Poland was founded in 1992. Its primary task is to work for full participation by Romani people in Polish public life. One of the Association's main goals is to recall and commemorate the extermination and the Holocaust of the Roma; this is accomplished through education, publishing, research and exhibitions. The Association also engages in many different activities aimed at overcoming negative stereotypes about Roma prevailing in Polish society.

Auschwitz-Birkenau Memorial and Museum in Oświęcim, Poland

http://www.auschwitz.org.pl

Languages: English, German, Polish

Before planning a class visit to Auschwitz-Birkenau, it is worth visiting the Museum's official web site. There one can find clearly presented or-

118

ganizational details (directions, accommodations, rules during visits, and visiting hours) and plainly written information on the history of the camp (establishment, expansion, the crematoria and gas chambers, number and nationalities of victims, liberation). The scope of information seems to exactly match the needs of secondary school students. Unfortunately the Museum archives are not yet accessible to Internet users, as work on computerizing the collections is in progress. The Education Department works with teachers and school youth, arranging lectures, training, museum lessons, competitions, etc. The Latest News section tells about changes at the Museum (e.g., newly opened visitor areas, new informational systems) and all kinds of observances and events connected with Museum activities. The site also presents the Museum's publications, including academic works, popular works, literature, albums, guides, catalogues, posters, post cards and educational films, but they cannot be purchased on-line. There is information on the Auschwitz-Birkenau Death Camp Victims Memorial Foundation, which supports the Museum.

Also functioning in Oświęcim are these organizations: the International Youth Meeting House (www.mdsm.pl); the Center for Dialogue and Prayer, headed by Rev. Manfred Deselaers (www.centrum-dialogu.oswiecim.pl); and the Auschwitz Jewish Center Foundation (www.ajcf.org).

These institutions organize several-day sessions for youth groups, involving historical, religious and civic education.

Beit Warszawa
http://www.beit-warszawa.org.pl
Languages: English, Polish (English sections less current)
The Beit Warszawa Jewish Cultural Association is a progressive, egalitarian Jewish social organization. *Beit* is Hebrew for "home." Beit Warszawa is a home open to everyone who wishes to participate in building the progressive Jewish community in Warsaw and across Poland. The creation of

a Jewish community means participating in all aspects of Jewish spiritual, cultural, secular and religious life. It is for those searching for their path in Judaism or who wish to broaden their knowledge of the culture and history of the Polish Jews. The Beit Warszawa site has information on observances of Jewish holidays and other events organized by the Association.

Beyond the Pale. The History of Jews in Russia

http://www.friends-partners.org/partners/beyond-the-pale

Languages: English, Russian

This is the on-line version of the original 1995 exhibition shown in Russia. It shows the history of the Jews in Europe and Russia, their daily life and religion. Its purpose is to convey the great danger posed by intolerance and prejudice, by showing the anti-Jewish myths that accumulated through the centuries, and the discrimination and isolation that led to the Holocaust. The exhibition consists of archive photographs, drawings, pictures and documents, accompanied by brief notes. The exhibition is easy to navigate. The material is divided into subject blocks: The Middle Ages, The Development of Modern Anti-Semitism, Jews in the Russian Empire, Jews in the Soviet Union, Nazism and the Holocaust, 1941 to the Present, and Democracy and Minority Rights. Particularly worth attention is some rarely presented material: propaganda posters, caricatures and medieval frescos.

Center for Culture and Dialogue

http://www.ignatianum.edu.pl

Languages: English (part), Polish (part)

The Center for Culture and Dialogue was established at the Ignatianum College of Philosophy and Education in Cracow. It was founded by Polish Jesuits in 1998 and is directed by Professor Stanisław Obirek SJ. Its goal is to bring distant cultures closer and to find a platform for understanding. The Center also conducts research. The site presents news and statements from the point of view of the Catholic Church, and the work of Jesuits on behalf of Christian-Jewish dialogue.

The site contains information on academic seminars the Center organizes (e.g., Toward Better Familiarity, or, On Polish-Israeli Relations), publications (e.g., *The Cross and the Star of David* [in Polish] by Professor Jan Grosfeld) and conferences to promote dialogue (e.g., Jesuits and Jews: Towards Greater Fraternity and Commitment). The reports from academic seminars are supplemented by transcripts of some speeches.

Center for Holocaust and Genocide Studies
http://www.chgs.umn.edu
Language: English
The Center for Holocaust and Genocide Studies is an academic institution operating under the auspices of the University of Minnesota. Its goal is to further Holocaust research. It studies not only the Nazi crimes against the Jews, but also other genocides that took place in the 20th century. The Center addresses such problems as the massacre of Armenians in 1915, Nazi medical experiments on human beings, and the situation of Roma and Sinti, Poles, Jehovah's Witnesses, homosexuals and other victims of nazism.

Center for Holocaust, Genocide & Peace Studies
http://www.unr.edu/chgps/blank.htm
Language: English
The Center for Holocaust, Genocide & Peace Studies operates at the University of Nevada, Reno. It is engaged in studies of the Holocaust, prejudice, and contemporary ethnic conflicts. Besides offering a number of courses to the University's students, the Center cooperates on the making of documentary and feature films on the Holocaust. Award-winning films can be purchased at the site. It also has an archive of related articles.

Cybrary of the Holocaust

http://www.remember.org

Language: English

This is a very extensive but user-friendly site that covers many subject areas, set up by the Alliance for a Better Earth. It consists of several sections. One is a virtual library of more than 2,000 titles on the Holocaust, with many items accessible at the site. Articles and reviews of new publications are in a separate section.

The Education section has a comprehensive set of materials for classroom activities, and promotes exchange of experiences and ideas (e.g., reports of experiments and alternative teaching methods).

The site also has a section devoted to art inspired by the Holocaust, including works by survivors. There is a special Children of Survivors section where feelings can be shared and the effect of the Holocaust on the postwar history of families can be described. The fate of some of the people who disappeared during the war is still unknown today. The Search and Unite section provides help with searches and also in recovering lost property. The site is updated monthly.

David's Holocaust Awareness Project

http://members.aol.com/dhs11/remember.html

Language: English

The author of the site is 11-year-old David from New Jersey, who wrote what he learned about the Holocaust. David encourages the reader to learn more about the subject so that no similar events will take place anymore. The site contains photographs and links to the most important sites about the Holocaust. More of the photographs David used can be found at http://www.fmv.ulg.ac.be./schmitz/holocaust.html

Forum for Dialogue Among Nations

http://www.dialog.org.pl

Languages: English, Polish

This foundation aims to create a climate of tolerance and promote democratic values, and to draw together the peoples that through the centuries have coexisted in Poland and have co-created its history, tradition and culture. By presenting the little-known histories of the town of Gliwice and the Silesia region, it hopes to encourage coexistence without stereotypes, prejudice and fear. In its educational activities the foundation focuses on youth. Ongoing projects include "Meetings on the Borderland," a series of meetings to familiarize Silesians with the culture and issues of particular national minorities, and two-day retreats for tolerance workshops for high school students, with simulation games, tests and psychological games to engage participants with issues of tolerance, stereotypes, and life in a multicultural society. Another interesting initiative was an academic session on the history of Silesian Jews, commemorating the 60th anniversary of Kristallnacht. The web site contains well-developed educational resources for teachers and students, as well as links to other Polish sites devoted to tolerance and multicultural education. The web site provides an opportunity for students and teachers to participate in Polish-Jewish dialogue, and a discussion forum in English.

Forum – Jews – Poles – Christians
Znak Foundation for Christian Culture

http://www.znak.com.pl/forum

Languages: English, Polish

This site is intended to foster cooperation between Christians and Jews. It was created with assistance from the Polish Council of Christians and Jews and from EuroDialog, an Internet service devoted to intercultural dialogue. The site has pages of information and reflections on Polish-

Jewish relations, exchange of experiences, and presentations of new proposals. The site is updated continually with current events and an extensive review of the press. The Viewpoint section features statements by journalists and clerics, especially those involved in promoting dialogue and understanding. The Znak Foundation lets young people speak through, for example, its "Why Auschwitz, Kolyma, Kosovo?" competition. Students can learn the views and feelings of their peers and can familiarize themselves with the chronicle of those tragic events and with art inspired by them. The site is also a source of information on other institutions promoting dialogue.

Gedenkstätten für NS-Opfer in Deutschland
http://www.topographie.de/gedenkstaettenforum/uebersicht
Languages: English, French, German
This web site, prepared by the Stiftung Topographie des Terrors (Topography of Terror Foundation) of Berlin, has well-designed interactive maps of the places of Nazi terror (camps, etc.) in the Federal Republic of Germany, grouped by their names and locations. The descriptions give basic historical and bibliographical data, information on visiting hours and conditions, and links to other sites related to the listed place.

Ghetto Fighters' House
Holocaust and Jewish Resistance Heritage Museum – Israel
http://www.gfh.org.il
Languages: English, Hebrew
The Ghetto Fighters' House was founded in 1949 by surviving ghetto fighters and partisans in Western Galilee. It was the world's first Holocaust document archive. Soon it began to function as a museum, research institute and educational center. It forms a community of people who survived the Holocaust, tells their stories and passes on their message. The basic

units of it are the Ghetto Fighters' House, the Yad Layeled Children's Memorial Museum, archive, library and educational center.

The site presents the permanent historical and documentary exhibitions on the life of Jews before the Holocaust, their fate during the Holocaust, resistance and uprisings. It describes a unique collection of works of art made in the camps and ghettos, and postwar art inspired by the Holocaust.

Yad Layeled is dedicated to the memory of the child victims of the Holocaust. It is intended for young visitors. Museum visits include art workshops, film showings, dramas, and meetings with witnesses to the Holocaust. The Museum's Janusz Korczak International School runs the International Book-Sharing Project, a cooperative effort between schools in Israel and other countries involving exchange of views on Holocaust literature. The Internet site provides a means to join the project.

The site's Archives have an enormous collection with a search facility. Library staff offer assistance in compiling bibliographies.

The Educational Section and Overseas Department organize seminars and training for groups of teachers and students from different countries. The Pedagogical Resource Center consists of two sections helping students and teachers. The site also has a section devoted to Janusz Korczak.

Grodzka Gate NN Theater Center
http://www.tnn.lublin.pl
Language: Polish
The Center is a local government cultural institute in Lublin, working for the preservation of cultural heritage and for education. In its programs the Center invokes the symbolic and historical meaning of its site, the Grodzka Gate (formerly the gate separated the Christian and the Jewish towns), as well as the city of Lublin, a meeting place of cultures, traditions and religions.

The NN Theater was founded in 1990. At first it was strictly a theater, but with the passing of time it opened up to other social and educational activities. The Center remodeled its headquarters, the 14th-century Grodzka Gate and adjoining buildings, reinvigorating this part of Lublin's old city center. The Center's program activities are connected with perpetuating the memory of the Jewish town through artistic activities, exhibitions, meetings, sessions, the promotion of books and magazines, films, concerts and social activities. It also runs a publishing house. In 1998 the Center began a program entitled "The Great Book of the City" in which archive materials connected with the Polish-Jewish history of Lublin (photographs, oral history, documents) are gathered. Those materials were used to create an exhibition showing the prewar bicultural city of Lublin, accompanied by an educational program devoted to preserving the heritage of the Lublin Jews. The Center also runs a cultural heritage program entitled "The Forgotten Past: The Multicultural Traditions of Lublin and its Region," addressed mainly to young residents and their teachers. Another project is "The Virtual Library of Lublin and Surrounding Regions," a computer database with texts, pictorial material, sound, and educational tools.

The Center cooperates with teachers through the "Roads of the Past" School Discovery Club, with a network of almost 100 clubs around the entire Lubelskie Province. In 2001 the Center hosted the Education for Reconciliation workshop organized by the Carnegie Council of New York and the Jagiellonian University's Department of Judaic Studies.

Haus der Wannsee-Konferenz. Gedenk- und Bildungsstätte
http://www.ghwk.de
Languages: Chinese, Czech, English, French, German, Hebrew, Italian, Polish, Russian, Spanish, Swedish, Turkish
The Wannsee Conference House Memorial and Educational Center is located in the building where, on January 20, 1942, leading officials of

the Third Reich finalized the organizational details to implement an earlier decision to deport the Jews of Europe to the east and murder them en masse. Since 1992 the building has served as a memorial and a center for historical education. The site briefly describes the institution's work: a museum exhibition about the Wannsee Conference and the Jewish Holocaust; a media library that contains books, documents, microfilms and videos; and one-day or several-day educational programs for youth and adults. In regard to the latter, the educational department works with schools. The site also contains the protocols of the Wannsee Conference, with English and Polish translations. There is a well-prepared section of links grouped by country and subject.

Holocaust History Project

http://www.holocaust-history.org

Language: English

This site is an archive of Holocaust-related documents, photographs, recordings and essays. It also contains materials for combatting Holocaust denial. There are answers given for even detailed questions. A virtue of the site is that it not only gives information about documents but allows original photos of them to be printed, with transcriptions and English translations. There is an alphabetical keyword index to questions that were sent electronically to, and answered by, specialists dealing with Holocaust subjects. New questions can be answered in the same way.

Holocaust Memorial Center

http://www.holocaustcenter.org

Language: English

The Center, located in Farmington Hills, Michigan, was established at the initiative of Rabbi Charles H. Rosenzveig in 1981. Its mission is to perpetuate the memory of the culture and way of life of the Jews murdered during the Holocaust, to point out the indifference of those who did nothing to prevent it, to present the richness of the culture of European Jews, and to help future generations to create a free, open society.

The site contains a historical section describing the period from the beginnings of nazism in Germany to the end of the war, with a chronological review of events illustrated by many archival photographs. It provides access to a very extensive English- and German-language Internet bookstore grouped by subject. The Museum Exhibits On-line section invites visitors to the Holocaust Memorial Center's exhibitions, but has no Internet access to them, except for the interactive Life Chance exhibition, which allows the site visitor to take on the role of a young educated Jew living in Nazi Germany and make crucial decisions. The program shows the hopelessness of all actions and the Jews' powerlessness during that time.

Holocaust Museum & Studies Center
http://www.bxscience.edu/organizations/holocaust
Language: English
The Museum was established at the Bronx High School of Science in 1977, and is one of the oldest institutions of its kind in the United States. It also boasts close cooperation with Nobel laureates Elie Wiesel and Simon Wiesenthal. The site allows viewing of a small part of the Museum's rich collection, including propaganda posters from World War II and works by artists who survived the Holocaust. The Holocaust Educational Guide section contains ready lesson plans, suggestions for innovative exercises, brief historical descriptions of the most important issues connected with the Holocaust, many maps, and methodological guidelines.

Holocaust Teachers Resources Center

http://www.holocaust-trc.org

Language: English

This web site was established by the Holocaust Education Foundation, Inc. The main purpose of the organization is to combat prejudice by disseminating knowledge of the Holocaust. The site collects and collates educational materials. Much space is devoted to lesson plans prepared for classes at different levels of education. They are described in great detail, in terms of methodology as well. The lessons often rely on specific books (the corresponding chapters can be accessed at the site). Many types of educational materials are described in the following sections: videos on the Holocaust, a guide to educational materials (an extensive catalogue of books and audio and video cassettes, grouped by subject), and a guide to literature about the fate of children during World War II (diaries, memoirs, history books, documents, literature and encyclopedias).

The Holocaust: A Tragic Legacy

http://library.thinkquest.org/12663

Language: English

The site is edited by students in ThinkQuest, an organization that promotes Internet learning. Its basic virtue is interactivity. The site visitor has opportunities to solve moral dilemmas, take part in a virtual Nuremberg trial, test his or her knowledge in one of the five quizzes, and observe life in a virtual concentration camp. The site also has a chronological review of events from 1933 to 1945, connected with a glossary of the most important Holocaust-related terms. The site's attractive visual design and original way of communicating knowledge make it particularly interesting to youth.

iEARN – The Holocaust/Genocide Project

http://www.iearn.org/hgp/

Language: English

The International Education and Resource Network is a program for students from ages 12 to 17, involving schools from all over the world, including Poland. It relies on communication possibilities offered by the Internet: on-line discussion and e-mail. It also has workshops and annual world conventions of the participants. The site covers many interdisciplinary topics, including a subject block on the Holocaust and other genocides. Within the iEARN framework, teachers can take advantage of innovative exercises employing literature, history and art. Students taking part in the program edit the *An End to Intolerance* annual magazine, the whole of which is Internet-accessible. It enables the web site visitor to learn the views and feelings of young people from all over the world about the Holocaust. The site has a rich collection of links to other sites devoted to the Holocaust.

Janusz Korczak

http://www.janusz-korczak.de

Language: English (2 items), German

The site is dedicated to the life and legacy of Janusz Korczak. It contains his biography, a list of German and English literature on his life and work, and information on translations of his writings in those languages. The site presents the pillars of Korczak's educational practice of respect for the rights of the child, based on the principle that adults' respect for the child teaches the child to be cognizant of other people.

There is a list of institutions in Germany that bear Janusz Korczak's name. Also provided are Holocaust-related links. The English items are a speech by Yitzhak Rabin in Warsaw and a complete play about Janusz Korczak.

130

Jewish Historical Institute

http://www.jewishinstitute.org.pl

Languages: Polish

The Institute, which traces its beginnings to 1928, is engaged in research and education on the history and culture of the Jews in Poland. The headquarters in Warsaw houses a large archive and a varied collection of art and artifacts of Jewish culture. The daily work of the Institute involves protecting, preserving, completing, exhibiting and studying its collection of documentary and other material. It also organizes seminars, conferences, competitions and a Hebrew language course. All departments are committed to filling gaps in the public's knowledge, countering stereotypes, and opposing prejudiced opinions resulting from ignorance. Particularly useful for Holocaust studies is the archive: among its prewar, wartime and postwar holdings are 7,200 survivor accounts, which, as the web site text emphasizes, all deserve the attention that a few well-known accounts have received.

The web site opens with a schedule of upcoming lectures. The web site describes the Institute's three permanent exhibitions, which show the life and death of the Warsaw ghetto, photographs and documents from the Ringelblum Archive, and Jewish sacral and secular art. There is also a catalogue of the library's collection of 70,000 items; material may be used in the library or photocopies may be requested. The bookstore's many books for sale are listed; orders can be placed by post or e-mail.

Jews in Poland. To Save from Oblivion. To Educate for the Future.

http://www.historiazydow.edu.pl

Languages: Polish (German and English site maps)

The organization is an educational service for teachers and students, providing basic information on Jewish history and culture, and materials for teaching tolerance. The web site aims to make young people aware of cultural, ethnic, religious and political diversity. The service was founded in cooperation with the Anne Frank Museum in Amsterdam, the Stefan Batory Foundation, the Dutch Embassy in Warsaw and the Polish-German Center Association (which coordinates and develops the service in Poland). The service has a 24-slide multimedia presentation on the Jews in Poland: past, present and future. Since 1998, the exhibition has been presented in dozens of Polish and German cities. The teachers' section has ready teaching materials, lesson plans and bibliographies. The service welcomes original teaching plans. The students' section encourages submission of opinions and thoughts on the subject matter, essays, and presentations of educational projects carried out in schools. There is information on competitions, seminars, teacher training, lectures and other events.

Judaica Foundation – Center for Jewish Culture

http://www.judaica.pl

Languages: Polish, English, German

The idea of creating the Judaica Foundation – Center for Jewish Culture was born in Cracow at the end of the 1980s, a time of historic changes in Poland. The idea emerged among people from the worlds of culture, education and the arts. The late President of the Jewish Congregation in Cracow, Czesław Jakubowicz, was actively involved in this civic initiative. The Foundation began its activities in 1991, and on November 24, 1993, the Center was opened under its auspices in a former house of prayer in Kazimierz, the old Jewish quarter of Cracow.

The main aims are to preserve the Jewish heritage, to perpetuate the memory of the centuries-long presence of the Jews in Poland, to disseminate knowledge of the history and culture of the Polish Jews among young people, to create a platform for Polish-Jewish dialogue, and to promote the values of an open civil society.

The Center's program, addressed to the Jewish and non-Jewish public from Poland and abroad, includes lectures, meetings with authors, book promotions, conferences and seminars, showings of documentary and feature films, concerts, exhibitions, and special summer programs.

The Center's Bayit Hadash (New Home) Encounters with Jewish Culture is a ten-week program packed with thematically grouped events, organized since 1996, beginning in the first month of the Jewish year – Tishri, during the High Holidays.

The Center's Aleksander and Alicja Hertz Annual Memorial Lecture is a series of lectures related to Polish-Jewish issues, subsequently published in Polish and English. Czesław Miłosz inaugurated the series in 1999, followed by Shoshana Ronen, Ryszard Kapuściński and Karl Dedecius.

Literature of the Holocaust

http://www.english.upenn.edu/~afilreis

Language: English

Al Filreis, Professor of English at the University of Pennsylvania, gives a bibliography of articles and other material about the Holocaust, with a list of links to related web sites.

Mordechaj Anielewicz Center
for Research and Education on Jewish History and Culture

http://www.centrum-anielewicza.uw.edu.pl

Language: Polish

The Mordechaj Anielewicz Center for Research and Education on Jewish History and Culture was founded in 1990 under an agreement between Warsaw University and the Jack Fliderbaum Foundation. Currently it functions as a unit in the Institute of History at Warsaw University. The Center conducts classes for history students and those from other faculties who are interested in the history and culture of the Polish Jews, with undergraduate and postgraduate programs. The Center also organizes regular field trips and seminars for historians and researchers. Publications by young historians and students are funded by the Irena Grabowska-Kruszewska and Enta Marmelstein-Kotkowska Foundation. On May 8, 2003, the Center organized the first Jewish Day at Warsaw University.

Museum of the History of Polish Jews

http://www.jewishmuseum.org.pl

Languages: English, Polish

The Museum of the History of Polish Jews web site is about a museum currently being created in Warsaw, devoted to the memory of the Polish Jews and financed by the Association of the Jewish Historical Institute in Poland. It is planned as a large center for exhibitions and educational activity, to supplement the collections and publishing activities of the Jewish Historical Institute. The Museum will present the history and culture of Polish Jews. Historians from Poland, Europe and the United States are involved, directed by Professor Israel Gutman of the Hebrew University in Jerusalem. Replicas, dioramas and models will be created. Over 40,000 artifacts have been located, photographed and computerized. The next stage is to search the eastern territories of Poland, Belarus, Ukraine, Russia and around the world, and to cooperate with Jewish museums in Europe, the United States and Israel that have many artifacts from Poland or connected with the history of Polish Jews. The web site has information on the project and a brief guide to the history of the Jews in Poland.

Nadzieja-Hatikvah Society

http://www.nadzieja-hatikvah.org

Languages: English, Polish

Students and academics of the Faculty of Social Sciences at the University of Wrocław founded the Polish-Israeli Nadzieja-Hatikvah Society in the autumn of 2000. It also functions as an academic club for interested students in the Institute of International Studies at the University of Wrocław.

The Society fosters contact between communities, social and educational organizations in Poland and Israel, and the Jewish minority in Poland. An important element in Hatikvah's activities is the fight against racial and ethnic prejudice among young people in Europe, especially in Wrocław. It introduces young people to the history and culture of minorities. The Society's interests include the history of the Jews in Europe and in Poland, the State of Israel, Polish-Israeli and Polish-Jewish relations, and multicultural education. The Society organizes and participates in open discussions, meetings and lectures, international youth seminars, social work, workshops for students, and study trips. The Society also publishes *Hatikvah* twice per semester. Other important activities include the Minorities in Poland and Around the World lecture series, cooperation with the Education Ministry on student exchange programs with Israel, the Peace Education training course for teachers of multiculturalism, painting over and removing anti-Semitic and racist slogans around the city, and coordinating the volunteer work of young people from different countries in Jewish cemeteries and memorial sites.

Nizkor

http://www.nizkor.org

Languages: English, some sections in Spanish and Russian

Nizkor is Hebrew for "we will remember," and preserving the memory of the Holocaust is the main purpose of this site. It gives access to a rich collection of historical data, intelligibly grouped. Particularly useful is a section with 66 commonly asked questions about the Holocaust, and their answers.

Another section enables on-line purchases of teaching aids such as books, videos, posters and lesson plans. Many antiracist organizations and academic institutes dealing with the Holocaust can be contacted through the site.

Open Republic Association
Against Anti-Semitism and Xenophobia
http://or.icm.edu.pl
Language: Polish
Open Republic fights racism and xenophobia by initiating and promoting educational activities, documenting manifestations of prejudice, and making the public aware of them. The association aims to foster openness to and respect for those of different ethnic backgrounds, nationalities, religions, cultures or societies, and to oppose attitudes that undermine human dignity. The members of Open Republic are teachers, writers, journalists and the clergy. They disseminate information on the sources of xenophobia, anti-Semitism and racism, and bring them to the attention of government authorities, churches, teachers, scholars and the media. The association cooperates with the Helsinki Foundation for Human Rights, the Polish Humanitarian Campaign and the Never Again Association.

The Association's School of Openness project analyses and describes school textbooks in the humanities, with a view to whether their content promotes the idea of open civil society. The Open Republic site also has reviews of anti-Semitic or extreme nationalist publications.

Ronald S. Lauder Foundation in Poland
http://www.lauder.pl
Languages: English, Polish
The Polish office of the New York City-based Ronald S. Lauder Foundation opened in 1991. The main aims of the Foundation are to preserve and protect the Jewish cultural heritage in Poland, to conduct cultural and charitable activities for the Jewish community in Poland, to help meet their

cultural and religious needs, to support initiatives aimed at presenting the culture, history and tradition of the Jews in Poland, and to support activities that create new possibilities of Polish-Jewish dialogue, especially in cultural matters.

The Foundation's projects in Poland include a kindergarten, educational camps, primary schools, Hebrew language courses, youth clubs, a genealogical project, a yeshiva and publishing house, a journal, annual Jewish Book Days, and holiday observances. Guides and information packages in pdf. format can be found at the web site.

Shoa.de

http://www.shoa.de

Language: German

The site is part of a project that also addresses the Third Reich, the Second World War and the postwar years. It has four sections: Subjects (dozens of topics including anti-Semitism, Einsatzgruppen, ghettos, concentration camps, the Nuremberg laws and Zyklon B), Victims and Heroes, Perpetrators, and Sources (e.g., literature on Hitler, films and archival recordings).

The site does not have its own discussion forum, but links to Aktion Kinder des Holocaust (www.akdh.ch).

Shoah Project

http://www.shoahproject.org

Language: German

The Shoah Project site has several sections, introduced by News. The Documentation section has materials on the Dachau concentration camp, and a work by Dr. Rolf Kornemann, "Doppelmord," describing the Nazis' anti-Jewish policy on property and housing. The Resistance section contains information on manifestations of resistance to nazism in Germany (*Die weisse Rose* student movement, and a link to the *Kids im Nazi-Regime* site). The Internet section has Holocaust-related links, with a subsection "Uncensored Against Nazism." In the section devoted to literature there are stories, essays and poems on Holocaust subjects, and the bibliographical section gives information on new German books, reviews, and an extensive bibliography grouped by subject.

Simon Wiesenthal Center
http://www.wiesenthal.com
Language: English
The Simon Wiesenthal Center is an international organization engaged in promoting tolerance, defending human rights and preserving the memory of the Holocaust. The site has brief news items about terrorism and other manifestations of intolerance around the world, mostly from the Middle East, and also information on neo-Nazi groups and methods of opposing them. The Museum of Tolerance section relates to the Center's educational activity. The Special Collections contain thousands of text files and photographs describing the history of the Holocaust and World War II, virtual exhibits, and many articles and essays. The site has a bibliography prepared especially for teachers, and 36 important questions and answers about the Holocaust.

Survivors of the Shoah. Visual History Foundation
http://www.vhf.org
Language: English
The Foundation was established by Steven Spielberg in 1994. Its purpose is to collect eyewitness accounts of the Holocaust in the form of filmed documents on CD and video cassette. So far more than 50,000 accounts from 57 countries and in 32 languages have been collected. The site gives information about the project and the educational films made as a result.

Work is proceeding on cataloging the recordings and utilizing the archives for education in the classroom. The archive will be made available at the following institutions: the Fortunoff Video Archive for Holocaust Testimonies at Yale University, New Haven; the Museum of Jewish Heritage in New York City; the Simon Wiesenthal Center in Los Angeles; the United States Holocaust Memorial Museum in Washington, D.C.; and Yad Vashem in Jerusalem.

United States Holocaust Memorial Museum
http://www.ushmm.org
Language: English
The Museum was established in 1980 to study and interpret the history of the Holocaust. The site tells the user about the institution's wide-ranging research and educational activities, with information on current studies and access to part of the archives. Documents are also presented in some of the on-line exhibitions. The site offers educational material in sections geared to students, to families, to teachers, to adults, and to university students and scholars. These sections develop many Holocaust subjects: the situation of children and women, resistance, etc. Film of the liberation of Auschwitz can be viewed. Clearly written material for students recounts the history of nazism and the Holocaust. The material is supplemented by many photographs and maps, and a glossary of the most important terms. The section for teachers presents several books recommended for teaching about the Holocaust. A broad assortment of books can be purchased from the Museum's Internet shop.

Web's Center for Holocaust Education
http://www.hopesite.ca
Language: English
The site was created by the Victoria Holocaust Remembrance and Educa-

tion Society, a Canadian organization. It has three main sections: Remember, Reflect, and Rekindle.

"Remember" is a collection of Holocaust survivor memoirs (interviews, video recordings, diaries). One section is devoted to childhood during the Holocaust.

"Reflect" is where anyone can post an opinion, poem or other reflection. Here there is also a special section for helping the children of Holocaust survivors (support groups, therapy groups, etc.). There is also a link with a guide to Holocaust-related web sites.

"Rekindle" speaks of the need to build hope. It suggests actions anyone can undertake against intolerance, prejudice and racism. It also raises issues such as racism in schools, human rights, understanding other cultures, and teaching about the Holocaust.

Yad Vashem

http://www.yad-vashem.org.il

Languages: English, Hebrew

The Yad Vashem Memorial Institute in Jerusalem is one of the best-known institutions dealing with the Shoah. The wide-ranging site reflects the Institute's many areas of activity. The About Yad Vashem section contains detailed information about its history, current activities and plans for the future. The section on the Holocaust has a list of questions most often asked and their answers, a chronology of events, a bibliography of more than 200 books considered most important by scholars and teachers, hundreds of documents from that time (translated to English), and monographs on the Jewish communities of Grodno, Lida and Olkieniki. The Remembrance section contains biographies of victims. The Eleventh Hour Collection Project is intended to collect testimonies, documents and material evidence from private persons. The Commemorating the Names project gathers the names and biographical details of victims. The On-Line Exhibitions section presents 13 interesting exhibitions from the Museum collections. Especially moving is "No Child's Play," about the fate of children during the Holocaust.

Yad Vashem has much experience in teaching about the Holocaust. In the Education section one can find general guidelines and pointers, and information on workshops for teachers and on conferences. There is also a Pedagogical and Resource Center with a range of educational aids and e-mail contacts. The Research and Publications section presents current research projects of the Institute and also offers the latest publications (Yad Vashem Publications) and lesson materials (Teaching Units) for sale.

The Righteous Among the Nations section gives biographies, photographs of memorial sites, and statistics about those who took great risks to save the lives of Jews during the Holocaust.

YIVO Institute for Jewish Research
http://www.yivoinstitute.org

Language: English

The YIVO Institute was established in 1925 in Vilnius as a center for research on the history and culture of the Jews in Eastern Europe. At present the Institute is continuing its activity in New York. It has an archive and a multilingual library, not accessible through the Internet. Available at the site are parts of photographic and documentary exhibitions, and a list of YIVO publications, some of which can be purchased through the Internet. The site provides a great amount of information about the Yiddish language, including an alphabet with audio of how the letters are pronounced.

About the Authors

Monika Adamczyk-Garbowska – Professor of American and comparative literature. Head of the Center for Jewish Studies, Marie Curie-Skłodowska University, Lublin. Translator of American and Yiddish literature. Member of the editorial staff of the annual *Polin: Studies in Polish Jewry*. Publications include *Polska Isaaca Bashevisa Singera: Rozstanie i powrót* (1994), *Contemporary Jewish Writing in Poland: An Anthology* (with A. Polonsky, 2001) and *Odcienie tożsamości. Literatura żydowska jako zjawisko wielojęzyczne* (2004). Recipient of the Jan Karski and Pola Nireńska Prize (2004) from the YIVO Institute for Jewish Research.

Natalia Aleksiun – Historian. Researcher at the Center for Near Eastern and Far Eastern Studies, Jagiellonian University, Cracow. Doctoral candidate in the Skirball Department of Hebrew and Judaic Studies, New York University. Recipient of the Prime Minister's Award (2002) for her 2001 doctoral thesis in the Faculty of History of Warsaw University. Publications include *Dokąd dalej. Ruch syjonistyczny w Polsce 1944–1949* (2002) and many articles on Polish-Jewish relations, the history of the Jews in Poland, and Jewish historiography.

Jolanta Ambrosewicz-Jacobs – Researcher at the Jagiellonian University Institute of European Studies, Cracow. Member of the OSCE/ODIHR Advisory Panel of Experts on Freedom of Religion or Belief, and its Working Group on Education for Tolerance. Member of the European Consortium for Political Research Standing Group on Extremism and Democracy. Publications include *Me – Us – Them. Ethnic Prejudice and Alternative Methods of Education: The Case of Poland* (2003) and *Tolerancja. Jak uczyć siebie i innych* (2003). Research interests include prejudice, anti-Semitism, intercultural education and reconciliation policy.

Olga Goldberg-Mulkiewicz – Professor at the Hebrew University, Jerusalem. Lecturer at the University of Łódź (1961–1967). From 1969, Lecturer and then Senior Lecturer in the Jewish and Comparative Folklore Program of the Hebrew University, and head of that program for many years. Research interests include Polish folk art; the Jews of Poland, Iraq and Yemen; and transformation and mutual borrowing in traditional Polish and Jewish culture.

Leszek Hońdo – Head of the Research Section on Jewish Culture in the Department of Judaic Studies of the Jagiellonian University, Cracow. Secretary of the Commission on the History and Culture of Polish Jews of the Polish Academy of Arts and Sciences. Chairman of the Committee for Protection of Monuments of Jewish Culture in Cracow. Publications include *Stary cmentarz żydowski w Krakowie* (1999), *Inskrypcje starego żydowskiego cmentarza w Krakowie* (2000) and *Cmentarz żydowski w Tarnowie* (2001). Recipient of the Jan Karski and Pola Nireńska Prize (2002) from the YIVO Institute for Jewish Research.

Tanna Jakubowicz-Mount – Psychotherapist in Warsaw. Cofounder of therapy centers: the Therapies and Personality Development Unit, the Psychoeducational Laboratory, and the Holistic Training Center. Leads the Polish Transpersonal Forum, which strives for the creative coexistence of people of different cultures, nationalities and spiritual traditions. Conducts "Meeting the Stranger" educational workshops.

Sławomir Kapralski – Sociologist. Faculty member, Centre for Social Studies of the Polish Academy of Sciences Institute of Philosophy and Sociology, Warsaw. Recurrent Visiting Professor at the Central European University, Budapest. Member of the European Association of Social Anthropologists. Co-organizer of educational programs at the Center for Jewish Culture in Kazimierz, Cracow. Publications include *Wartości a poznanie socjologiczne* (1995), *The Jews in Poland* (1999), *Reformulations: Markets, Policies, and Identities in Central and Eastern Europe* (2000) and *Democracies, Markets, Institutions: Global Tendencies in Local Contexts* (2002). Research interests include theory of culture, nationalism, ethnicity and changes in identity, anti-Semitism and Polish-Jewish relations, and the situation of Roma in Eastern Europe.

Sergiusz Kowalski – Sociologist. Faculty member, Polish Academy of Sciences Institute of Political Studies, Warsaw. Publications include *Krytyka solidarnościowego rozumu. Studium z socjologii myślenia potocznego* (1990), *Narodziny III Rzeczpospolitej* (1996), and Polish translations of Izaak Berlin, Timothy Garton Ash and Ralph Dahrendorf. Also writes for *Res Publika* and *Gazeta Wyborcza*. The recent *Zamiast Procesu. Raport o Mowie Nienawiści* (with M. Tulli, 2003) analyzes five right-leaning Polish newspapers. Research interests include analysis of political and public discourse, particularly the ideology of the right and extreme right.

Stanisław Krajewski – Faculty member, University of Warsaw Institute of Philosophy, specializing in logic and the philosophy of mathematics. Co-chairman of the Polish Council of Christians and Jews since its founding in 1989. Member of the Executive Committee of the International Council of Christians and Jews (1992–1998). Member of the Board of the Federation of Jewish Religious Community Councils in Poland since 1997.

Chairman of the Jewish Forum Foundation. Member of the International Council of the Auschwitz-Birkenau State Museum. Polish consultant to the American Jewish Committee. Publications include *Żydzi, judaizm, Polska* (1997), *Twierdzenie Gödla i jego interpretacje filozoficzne: od mechanicyzmu do postmodernizmu* (2003), *54 komentarze do Tory dla nawet najmniej religijnych pośród nas* (2004), and articles on Judaism, Jewish history and Christian-Jewish dialogue.

Ireneusz Krzemiński – Sociologist (proponent of humanistic sociology) and journalist. Professor at Warsaw University. Head of the Section on Theory of Social Change of the Warsaw University Institute of Sociology. Fellow of the Kościuszki Foundation. Prorector of the J. Giedroyc College of Communication and Media, Warsaw. Board Member of the Polish Pen Club. Member of the Advisory Board of the Polish Journalists' Association Press Freedom Monitoring Center. Publications include *Socjologia i symboliczny interakcjonizm* (1996), *Bitwa o Belweder* (with M. Grabowska, 1991), *Czy Polacy są antysemitami?* (1996), *Co się dzieje między ludźmi?* (1992), *"Solidarność" – projekt polskiej demokracji* (1997), and *Druga rewolucja w małym mieście. Zmiana ustrojowa w oczach mieszkańców Mławy i Szczecinka* (with P. Śpiewak, 2001). Research interests include the Solidarity movement, anti-Semitism, xenophobia, national stereotypes and attitudes to social minorities, including sexual minorities.

Zdzisław Mach – Professor of sociology and social anthropology. Head of the Social Anthropology Section and of the Jagiellonian University Institute of European Studies, Cracow. Director of the Jagiellonian University Institute of Sociology (1991–1993), and Dean of its Department of Philosophy (1993–1999). Publications include *Kultura i osobowość w antropologii amerykańskiej* (1989), *Symbols, Conflict and Identity* (1993) and *Niechciane miasta: migracja i tożsamość społeczna* (1998).

146

Research interests include the cultural formation of identity, ethnicity and nationalism, migration, theory of culture, and European integration.

Bohdan Michalski – Philosopher. Professor at the Leon Koźmiński Academy of Entrepreneurship and Management, Warsaw, and the College of Social Psychology, Warsaw. Director of the Polish Institute in Stockholm and advisor to the Polish Embassy in Stockholm (1994–1997). Member of the Association of Polish Writers. Member of the Editorial Committee for the 24-volume critical edition of collected writings of Stanisław Ignacy Witkiewicz, and author of many works on his philosophical and aesthetic views. Recipient of the Reconciliation Award (1996) from the Jewish Community Council of Stockholm for his work to promote Christian-Jewish dialogue in Sweden through the "Jews and Christians: Who Is Your Neighbor After the Holocaust?" program. Research interests include reconciliation ethics and policy, tolerance, multiculturalism, universal human rights versus minority group rights, and experimental programs for teaching tolerance.

Andrzej Mirga – Ethnologist. Cofounder of the Association of Roma in Poland. Consultant to many international organizations. Chairman of the Council of Europe's Specialist Group on Roma. Chairman of the Project on Ethnic Relations Romani Advisory Council, Princeton, U.S.A. Fellow of the Kościuszki Foundation and the Rockefeller Foundation. Has lectured at the Jagiellonian University, Cracow, and Rutgers University, United States. Was the Jagiellonian University's first Romani student. Publications include *Cyganie. Odmienność i nietolerancja* (with L. Mróz, 1994), *The Roma in the Twenty-First Century: A Policy Paper* (with N. Gheorghe, 1997) and "Romowie – proces kształtowania się podmiotowości politycznej" (1998, in: P. Madajczyk (ed.), *Mniejszości narodowe w Polsce*).

Stanisław Obirek SJ – Philosopher, theologian. Lecturer at the Ignatianum College of Philosophy and Education, Cracow. Director of the Center for Culture and Dialogue. Rector of the Jesuit Seminary and College, Cracow (1994–1998). Former lecturer at Holy Cross College, Worcester. Editor-in-Chief of the quarterly *Życie Duchowe* (1994–2001). Publications include *Jezuitów w Rzeczypospolitej Obojga Narodów w latach 1564–1668* (1996), *Sezon dialogu. Rozmów dwadziescia trzy* (2002) and *Co nas łączy? Dialog z niewierzącymi* (2002).

Robert Szuchta – History teacher at High School LXIV, Warsaw, specializing in teaching about the Holocaust and the history of the Jews and other minorities on Polish soil. Member of the Educational Commission of the Polish Historical Society. Publications include articles on historical and methodological subjects related to multicultural education and teaching about the Holocaust. Editor of the educational supplement to *Mówią wieki* monthly. Member of the Program Council of the Open Republic Association Against Anti-Semitism and Xenophobia. Publications include *Holocaust. Program nauczania o historii i zagładzie żydów na lekcjach przedmiotów humanistycznych w szkołach* (with P. Trojański, 2000; the first Polish curriculum for Holocaust teaching) and *Holokaust: zrozumieć dlaczego* (with P. Trojański, 2003; the first Polish textbook on the subject). Recipient of awards for outstanding achievement in educational work from the Polish Ministry of Education (1995) and the Polcul Foundation, Australia (2000).

Jerzy Tomaszewski – Professor of history. Faculty member, Warsaw School of Economics. Faculty member, College of National Economy, Kutno. Faculty member, University of Warsaw (1970–2002). Member of the Academic Board of the Jewish Historical Institute, Warsaw (1970–1994). Founder and head of the Mordechaj Anielewicz Center for Research and Education on Jewish History and Culture of the Warsaw University Institute of History (1990–2001). Publications include many works on the economic and political history of Poland and Central European countries, and the history of minorities in Poland, among them *Z dziejów Polesia* (1963), *Gospodarka międzywojenna w latach 1918–1939*, v. I–IV (with Z. Landau, 1967–1969), *Historia gospodarcza Polski XIX i XX w.* (with Z. Landau and I. Kostrowicka, 1975), *Rzeczpospolita wielu narodów* (1985) and *Europa Środkowo-Wschodnia 1944–1968* (1992).

Hanna Węgrzynek – Historian. Assistant Professor at the Jewish Historical Institute, Warsaw. Publications include *Czarna legenda Żydów. Procesy o rzekome mordy rytualne w dawnej Polsce* (1999), a report on content about Jews in history textbooks entitled *Nauczanie o Żydach w polskich szkołach* (1999), and the dictionary *Historia i kultura Żydów polskich* (2000).

Stefan Wilkanowicz – Chairman of the Znak Foundation for Christian Culture, Cracow. Vice-Chairman of the National Council of Lay Catholics. Vice-Chairman of the International Council of the Auschwitz-Birkenau State Museum. Vice-Chairman of the Auschwitz-Birkenau Death Camp Victims Memorial Foundation. Editor-in-Chief of *Znak* monthly (1978–1994). Member of the Pontifical Council for the Laity (1985–1995). Chairman of the Catholic Intellectuals Club in Cracow for many years. Published in *Tygodnik Powszechny*.